Praise for *The Future of Work*

"There is zero obfuscation in *The Future of Work*. Jacob maps out precisely how organizations must adapt going forward, while inspiring employees and managers to do their best."

—Don Tapscott, bestselling author of 15 books, most recently *Macrowikinomics*

"Jacob's book is invaluable for organizations striving to provide effective environments for tomorrow's workforce. People are much more self-directed and self-motivated at work, and technology continues to enable our ability to interact, connect, and communicate. As a result, successful companies will understand the growing role for managers to become leaders and will learn how to leverage the 'freelancer economy,' where skilled individuals come together to complete projects and then move on to the next. Companies that understand how to create an environment where teams dynamically assemble, both internally and externally, will not only attract superior talent, but will also be in an excellent position to innovate."

—Stephen Hoover, CEO of PARC

"Jacob's book shows why and how the future of work compels a commitment to create a new type of organization."

—Peter Guber, CEO Mandalay Entertainment Group, *New York Times* bestselling author of *Tell to Win*, owner of the Golden State Warriors, and co-owner of the LA Dodgers

"The world of work is changing and many organizations are struggling to adapt. In *The Future of Work*, Jacob has outlined what organizations can do to remain relevant and competitive."

—Tony Hsieh, *New York Times* bestselling author of *Delivering Happiness* and CEO of Zappos.com, Inc.

"Jacob builds a powerful case for why we must rethink everything we know about work. *The Future of Work* includes examples, frameworks, and a set of guiding principles that any organization should follow not just to survive, but to thrive."

—Michael Todman, President, Whirlpool International

"The thing about change is that everyone believes it's something that the other person needs to do. Yet, to change anything, it must begin with us. The future of work will either happen to us or because of us. Jacob paves the way for each of us to change how we work with each step we take."

—Brian Solis, digital analyst, anthropologist, futurist, author of *What's the Future of Business?*

THE FUTURE OF WORK

Attract New Talent, Build Better Leaders, and Create
a Competitive Organization

JACOB MORGAN

For general information about our other products and services, please contact our Customer Care Department within the United States at (800) 762-2974, outside the United States at (317) 572-3993, or fax (317) 572-4002.

Wiley publishes in a variety of print and electronic formats and by print-on-demand. Some material included with standard print versions of this book may not be included in e-books or in print-on-demand. If this book refers to media such as a CD or DVD that is not included in the version you purchased, you may download this material at http://booksupport.wiley.com. For more information about Wiley products, visit www.wiley.com.

ISBN 978-1-118-87724-1 (cloth); ISBN 978-1-118-87729-6 (ebk);
ISBN 978-1-118-87725-8 (ebk)

Printed in the United States of America

10 9 8 7 6 5 4

To Alex, Jenny, Irena, and Mika.
Thousands of miles away
but always in my thoughts.

Contents

Acknowledgments

I dedicated my last book, *The Collaborative Organization*, to my fiancée, Blake Landau, who, by the time this book comes out, will be my wife, Blake Morgan. I wouldn't have been able to write this book without her ongoing encouragement and support. Blake spent many hours listening to my ideas, reading through these pages, and pushing me to think differently. Thank you and I love you!

I also owe a huge debt of gratitude to my business partner Connie, who helps run Chess Media Group and has been the primary driving force behind the FOWCommunity (dedicated to the future of work and collaboration) that we launched around the time of this book. She kept steering the business ship and moving us in the right direction. We've worked together for almost five years now and I can't imagine having a better business partner.

I owe a huge debt of gratitude to my family both near (in L.A.) and far (in Melbourne) who are always cheering me on and are always excited for me.

My dad David, my mom Ella, and my brother Josh, I love you all very much; thank you all of your encouragement and support.

I'd also like to thank Wiley for being great to work with and for giving me the opportunity to share my ideas around the future of work.

There have also been numerous people who I spoke with and interviewed for this book, my apologies if I forgot anyone. Thank you to Chris Hummel for your support and your time; I'm privileged to know you. Thank you to Dr. John Kotter, your work has inspired me for many years. Gary Hamel, your passion and ideas have helped push me to think differently. Guy Halfteck, thanks for the many introductions you helped facilitate.

Thank you to Dmitry Zhgenti, Inga Sumska, and the rest of the DevEngineering team for creating the many amazing visuals in this book and for building our fantastic community. Pita, thank you for your contribution to the visuals as well.

Thank you to Mark Howorth, Erik Brynjolfsson, Dan Pink, Bill McDermott, Moises Norena, Jennifer Englert, Lynanne Kunkel, Dan Schawbel, Ryan Carson, Shoshana Deutschkron, Lindsey Nelson, Richard Green, Lauren Schulte, Retha Nicholson, Pamela Montana, Peter Aceto, Natasha Mascarenhas, Jason Stirman, Thomas Fried, Pat Kwan, Annette Clayton, Venancio Figueroa, Jennifer Dudeck, Sophie Vandebroek, Jennifer Englert, Bill Mckee Bill Wohl, Jeff Fettig, Stephen Hoover, Peter Guber, Brian Solis, Michael Todman, Don Tapscott, Brad Smith, Jodi Maroney, Ichiro Kawasaki, John B. Veihmeyer, Kim Beddard-Fontaine, Tony Hsieh, Natalie Fine, and anyone else I may have forgotten. All of your contributions and support helped inspire me and create this book.

Thank you to all my friends and to all of the clients and supporters of Chess Media Group, all of you make writing books like this fun and rewarding!

Introduction

Rethinking Chess and Work

Ultimately, what separates a winner from a loser at the grandmaster level is the willingness to do the unthinkable. A brilliant strategy is, certainly, a matter of intelligence, but intelligence without audaciousness is not enough. Given the opportunity, I must have the guts to explode the game, to upend my opponent's thinking and, in so doing, unnerve him. So it is in business: One does not succeed by sticking to convention. When your opponent can easily anticipate every move you make, your strategy deteriorates and becomes commoditized.

—Garry Kasparov

You probably haven't heard of the soon-to-be 24-year-old Magnus Carlsen. He is perhaps one of the few world champions that many people have never heard of. By most accounts Carlsen is the world's greatest chess player alive (and perhaps even dead). The assumption is and always has been that chess is just a board game but it is indeed a mental and physical battle that can last for many hours as players contemplate infinite calculations on the board. Consider that there are more possible moves in a game of chess than there are atoms in the entire universe or seconds that have elapsed since the Big Bang. Now imagine how challenging it is to calculate through all of the possible combinations to make the next best move; clearly it's impossible for any human to consider all the possible moves. Hopefully this gives you some perspective as to how tough of a "game" chess can be.

Many people are familiar with chess legend Garry Kasparov, who dominated the chess world for decades and who famously played (and lost to) IBM's Deep Blue. But Magnus is a new breed of chess player from a different era. When Garry was champion his peak rating was at 2,851, Magnus's peak rating at the time of writing is 2,881 and he recently defeated five-time former world chess champion Viswanathan Anand who was around twice his age without losing a single game, thus becoming the new world champion. Garry and Magnus first played in 2004 when Magnus was just 12 years old. Everyone knew Magnus would end up being a superstar when that game (which everyone thought Kasparov would win) ended in an unexpected draw.

In 2012, *60 Minutes* ran a profile on Magnus, calling him the "Mozart" of chess. In the *60 Minutes* clip he was filmed playing simultaneous games against 10 other players on separate boards without being able to look at any of them. He's also been known to do a bit of modeling, as he did for Liv Tyler and the G-star clothing line.

Many, including Kasparov, describe this as a new era in chess. Similarly, we also see a new era in the world of work.

One of the reasons why Magnus is such a great chess player is because he challenges the traditional notions of chess. When positions are technically drawn he plays through them and finds winning combinations and when positions are seemingly lost he manages to save them. He embraces and thrives in new or complex positions and has a unique ability to adapt to what is in front of him. He goes against the traditional grain of chess and for that he is considered to be one of the greatest chess players to play the game despite the fact that he is just turning 24.

The approach that Magnus has toward chess—the ability to adapt, identify opportunities, and think outside of the "board"—is the same type of mentality that is required when thinking about the future of work. Actually, it's not just required, it's essential for the future of work.

Many organizations around the world today are in trouble. The world of work is changing around them while they remain stagnant. The larger the gap grows the greater the chance becomes that these organizations will not survive. However, organizations shouldn't just want to survive they must want to thrive and be competitive in a new rapidly changing world. To do this requires pioneering change, not waiting for tragedy or for a crisis to force change. The future workforce is bringing new attitudes and ways of work to which managers must adapt. This means that organizations must adapt to both employees and managers and, as of now, this is happening at a snail's pace, if at all. This is a book about adapting to that change.

We spend a large portion of our existence working, thinking about work, worrying about or stressing out about work. Even though the average work week should be around 40 hours many still work 50, 60, 70, or more hours every week. We plan our lives around work and for many of us work is the focal point around which everything else revolves. People are working so much that companies like investment banking giant Goldman Sachs are actually trying to discourage some employees from working on weekends. In the finance world it's not that unusual for people to work 100-hour weeks!

Recent data from the Bureau of Labor Statistics shows that the majority of us now spend more time working than we do sleeping, an hour more a day. Work is officially the single most time-consuming thing in our lives today, so it's important that we enjoy and care about what we do because we're going to spend most of our lives doing it.

Work is clearly a big deal, but how many times have you actually thought about the following—What is work? What is an employee? What is a manager? If you had to explain these things to someone who wasn't familiar with them, what would you say?

When most people think of "work" they typically of think of four things: employees, managers, organizations, and technology. However, we never really stop to think about what these words actually mean even though they encompass such a large part of our lives.

If you were to look up synonyms for "work," you would find words like: stress, drudgery, toil, and daily grind. For "employee" you get gems such as: cog, servant, slave, or desk jockey. If you look up "company" you get: gang, zoo, or horde. Finally, we have "manager," which sees synonyms such as: slavedriver, zookeeper, and boss. Basically we are all cogs, working for a slavedriver, as we go through our daily drudgery working for a gang. Wow, work really sucks!

These are the words and the associations that we have been using to think about and describe our companies for the past 10, 50, and 150-plus years. It's no wonder why organizations are having such a hard time trying to evolve and adapt; we have literally built our companies from the ground up with the notion that employees are just cogs and that work is drudgery! Now we are working against the grain to change the approaches and ways of thinking about work but it's like trying to stop a speeding freight train. The difference is that now the need for change has never been greater.

During my keynote presentations at conferences and events I often ask the audience to tell me some of the things that make them happy or things that they enjoy doing. I get answers like: family, sports, good food and wine, friends, and a host of others. But I can't recall an instance where someone ever said "work makes me happy," or "I enjoy my job." This is all going to change. It has to change.

In my first book, *The Collaborative Organization*, I laid out a detailed strategic framework for how organizations can become collaborative by connecting their people and information anywhere, anytime, and on any device. I explored everything from use case development and technology evaluation to employee adoption and sustaining these initiatives in the long term. It was filled with case studies and models that organizations can use to help them become more collaborative. That book was designed as a strategic guide for decision makers, leaders, and those involved with making their organization more collaborative on the inside.

However, in writing that book I realized that it was necessary to talk about the future of work from a broader perspective. The world of work was changing yet there wasn't a clear description of what that change looked like or what impact that change might have. Time and time again we hear that employees work in new ways, that managers are using outdated approaches, and that organizations have to change the way they operate. It seems as though everyone knows this. But what exactly are the changes that employees are bringing into the workplace? What do they look like? What are some of the outdated management practices being used today and what do new approaches look like? If organizations are to rethink how they are constructed and operate then what do those new ideas actually look like? These are the pieces that are missing, not the fact that change needs to happen but what that change actually looks likes for employees, managers, and organizations and how to make that change happen.

I wanted to write a book to really help further the conversation around the future of work to get people thinking differently. That's what this book is about. Unlike my previous book, this is not a strategy guide with many models and frameworks, it's a compass to help guide organizations or a picture to help readers see what the future of work is going to look like.

In addition to this book my team and I at Chess Media Group also launched an invite-only membership community dedicated to the future of work and collaboration at FOWCommunity.com. The community not only allows you to share best practices and learn from other practitioners but it also provides members with access to regularly updated resources such as white papers, webinars, case studies, and research reports. Members of the community also get access to me and my team. Our goal is to help organizations adapt to the future of work and become more successful with their collaboration initiatives.

Many of us can sense and see how the world of work is changing but we aren't really sure why these changes are happening, what these changes mean, and how they are going to impact us. Hopefully that will change after reading this book.

Why can't you pick the projects or the teams that you work on? Why can't you use your own devices to get work done? Why can't you pick when and where you work? Why doesn't your manager ever show emotion? Why are semi-annual reviews the standard for evaluating performance? Why is your organization so hell-bent on maintaining such a strict hierarchy? I was always fascinated with these types of things and this fascination grew as I continued to consult with and research large and small organizations around the world. After all, if the world is changing so rapidly it would stand to reason that the way we think about and approach work should change as well . . . right?

Readers find that this book does not focus on consumers or customers but is instead centered on employees, an idea that was very much espoused by Vineet Nayar, the former CEO of HCL Technologies, in his book *Employees First, Customers Second: Turning Conventional Management Upside Down*. I acknowledge that customer centricity and customers in general are a crucial part of how businesses operate but change has to come from the inside first. I wanted to explore what that change looks like. In addition, I didn't want to take an overly futuristic approach by trying to paint a picture of work that might be too distant. Instead the focus is on the next three to six years, something tangible and relevant. Things are moving so quickly that trying to predict or assume anything beyond that time frame is just not realistic or practical.

This book is essentially broken down into three components that explore the future employee, the future manager, and the future company. Each one of these areas focuses on specific principles that comprise that area of the book. These principles can be viewed as action items or guiding posts for you and your organization. I encourage you to add to them, adapt them, and discuss them with your team. I've always been a fan of the descriptive approach to solving problems instead of the prescriptive approach, which assumes that all companies are the same and can follow the same steps. That is never the case.

The book is broken down into 12 chapters. The first chapter sets the stage outlining the key trends that are helping shape the future of work. Chapters 2 through 4 explore how employees currently work today and how the employee of the future will work. The meat of these chapters is based around the seven principles of the future employee, which are found in Chapter 3. These principles include flexible work environments, learning and teaching at will, and the idea that any employee within an organization has the opportunity to become a leader without having to be a manager. Chapter 4 introduces and explains the freelancer economy, which sees many individuals around the world making a living without being considered traditional employees. Many companies tap into this network of individuals.

Chapters 5 through 7 explore the current state of management today as well as outdated management practices that are still common in organizations today. Chapter 6 introduces the 10 principles of the future manager, which includes leading by example, following from the front, embracing vulnerability, and being a fire starter. Chapter 7 concludes this section on management with an exploration of how future managers are going to make their way into organizations.

Chapter 8 paints a picture of today's organizations and the challenges that many of them are currently going through, while Chapter 9 highlights the 14 principles of the future organization. Topics such as focusing on want instead of need, operating like a small company, seeing more women in senior management roles, and flatter company structures are all discussed here. Chapter 10 addresses the role of collaboration technology in the future organization as a central nervous system and explores the 12 habits of highly collaborative organizations. The discussion around the future organization concludes in Chapter 11 with the four roadblocks that most organizations are faced with when trying to adapt and evolve. Chapter 11 also introduces the six-step process that organizations can follow to adapt to the future of work. The book concludes in Chapter 12 by challenging readers to rethink what it means to work, to be an employee, to be a manager, or to run an organization.

At the end of the day, if your organization doesn't think about and plan for the future of work then your organization will have no future.

For those of you who want to connect with me directly you can do so by: emailing me at Jacob@ChessMediaGroup.com, connecting with me on twitter at https://www.Twitter.com/JacobM, or by visiting my site TheFutureOrganization.com. I look forward to hearing from you!

CHAPTER 1

The Five Trends Shaping the World of Work

Before examining anything around the future of work it's important to look at some of the key trends we are seeing today and how they are impacting the future of work. There are dozens of trends and shifts that are happening, but I have included in Figure 1.1 what I believe to be the most relevant and impactful to the world of work.

As you can see in Figure 1.1 the five trends shaping the future of work are:

1. New behaviors
2. Technology
3. Millennials
4. Mobility
5. Globalization

Let's take a look at each one in more detail to see how these trends are actually impacting the future of work.

THE FIVE TRENDS
SHAPING THE FUTURE OF WORK

1
NEW BEHAVIORS
Shaped by social media
& the web

2
TECHNOLOGIES
Shift to the cloud
Collaborative technologies
Big data
The Internet of things

3
THE MILLENNIAL
WORKFORCE
New attitudes,
expectations, & ways
of working

4
MOBILITY
Work anytime,
anywhere, & on
any device

5
GLOBALIZATION
No boundaries

© Chess Media Group

FIGURE 1.1   **The Five Trends Shaping the Future of Work**

NEW BEHAVIORS BEING SHAPED BY SOCIAL TECHNOLOGIES THAT ARE ENTERING OUR ORGANIZATIONS

Within the past 5 to 10 years we have seen a dramatic shift in our behavior. We share our company history and resumes on LinkedIn, we write blogs for the world to read on WordPress, we build communities and connect with people on Facebook, we search for and review companies on Yelp, we tell people where we are on Foursquare, and we can instantly find anything we are looking for on Google. These are new behaviors shaped by new technologies. If someone told you 10 years ago that you would be sharing so much information about yourself online for the world to see, you'd probably tell them that they were crazy. Yet look at where we are today. We share absolutely everything and this even extends to physical goods. We are opening up and becoming more collaborative. This isn't just a millennial thing either; this is a trend we are seeing across all demographics and geographies around the world.

Essentially we are much more comfortable living a public, collaborative, and connected life where we can connect and engage with people and information however we want. But therein lies the problem and the opportunity.

These new behaviors are now entering our organizations and this has given rise to new social and collaborative platforms for business. We are all very used to legacy intranets, email, CRM systems, billing and invoicing solutions, time-tracking technologies, and the like. However, we have never before had these new types of social and collaborative platforms enter our organizations.

The gap between what is called the *consumer web* and *enterprise* is large. The behaviors and the technologies that we use in our personal lives are quite different from the behavior and the technologies that we subscribe to in our companies.

If it's so easy for us to do the things mentioned earlier in our personal lives, then shouldn't it be just as easy to do those things in our professional lives? Why do we need to get 250 emails a day, why can't we find the right people and information we need to get work done? Why is there so much content duplication? Why can't we easily share, collaborate, and build communities with our coworkers? Why can't we crowdsource ideas?

These new behaviors and expectations are a key driving force that many organizations around the world are trying to adapt to and they are largely being fueled by the new behaviors we are seeing in our personal lives today.

Impact summary: New employee behaviors entering organizations are challenging the conventional idea of how employees work and what they expect from an organization.

TECHNOLOGY

There are many fascinating things happening in the world of technology that are dramatically starting to impact the way we work. The primary parts of technology that are impacting how we work are the shift to the cloud and collaboration platforms. However, it still remains to be seen what the impact of the *Internet of things* and big data will be on how we work. There are a few reasons for this. The first is that it's still a bit early to see what the impact of big data and the Internet of things will have on the workplace and while some organizations are thinking about or experimenting with these ideas, the vast majority are not. Out of all the trends, these are the two things that reside farthest on the fringes. They also operate more behind the scenes versus some of the other trends such as globalization, which are foremost in changing how we work and affect behavior. So although big data and the Internet of things might impact something such as how we share work or how customized work is created, it doesn't affect the fact that these things are happening to begin with. Automation and the introduction of artificial intelligence and robots into the workplace is another part of technology that could be discussed. However, it's too early to look at the impact of those tools in the workplace, at least for the purpose of this book.

Shift to the Cloud

The easiest way to think of the cloud is the Internet (or at least it serves the purpose for this book). The cloud powers many things that don't require any resources on the part of the user. Twitter, Facebook, LinkedIn, and probably any other piece of popular software you can think of is all powered by the cloud, no installation or assembly required. You just connect to the Internet and you're good to go.

Now this is important because typically when most organizations want to deploy a piece of technology it has to be done on the premises. In other words, some sort of physical installation needs to happen on the company site. This process can take a few days, a few weeks, or in some cases a few months. Then you have to deal with configuration, testing, and a whole mess of other issues. These deployments are regulated and controlled by specific management, HR, or IT teams that make technology decisions on behalf of everyone else in the company. The frustrating thing here for many employees is that the people who are purchasing the technologies oftentimes aren't the same people who are using them.

Then as new technologies or features are created there is a huge lag between when they are released versus when the organization actually deploys them. On average I see a one- to two-year lag between when something becomes available and when a company actually upgrades to the latest version of something. This is a huge gap, there's a lot that can happen in this time period.

Now that we can deploy cloud-based software within our companies we have eliminated the need for any type of physical installation. In fact, anyone can be up and running with the highest grade of business collaboration software in about the same amount of time as it takes to set up a Facebook page or buy something on Amazon. All you need is a credit card. This means that any employee within any company has the ability to select and deploy technology regardless of IT, legal, or corporate approval. The great thing is that as the vendor rolls out new features or upgrades, they get rolled out to the company as well, no more delay.

This is a radical shift for organizations as it now places the power in the hands of the employees. I was at a conference a few months ago and after my keynote a lady approached me and told me an interesting story. She handles accounting and invoicing at her company and they use an old in-house technology. The problem is the technology doesn't allow her to do everything she wants and often she is forced to spend hours trying to figure out workarounds. She was fed up with this and went on a search for a better solution. For $80 a month she found a platform that met all of her needs and was able to get up and running with it in just a matter of minutes. She solved her own problem and didn't ask anyone else about it. That's the power of the cloud.

However, this also creates a challenge because companies are see-ing a flurry of new technology deployments that they are essentially powerless to stop! Employees are taking matters into their own hands.

Impact summary: Technology decisions are now in the hands of anyone and everyone within an organization, not just IT or management. Cloud-based technologies should decrease the time to deploy, make upgrades and deployments easier and faster, and allow organizations to put together their own "stacks" made up of components from various vendors.

Collaboration Platforms

You may have heard of Jive, Yammer, Mango Apps, tibbr, Citrix, Clarizen, Bunchball, SAP Jam, Connections, Chatter, and the hundreds of other collaborative technologies that are out there. All of these technologies are connecting and engaging our people and information in ways that were never before possible—even just a few short years ago. As mentioned earlier, all of these technologies have been modeled after many of the popular platforms we use in our personal lives.

These new technologies have enabled employees to do things in a more effective and efficient way. Take, for example, a situation in which you needed to find someone in your company with a particular set of skills.

The usual approach here would be to send out an email asking your peers if they know of someone who can do XYZ. This action sets off a series of emails cascading throughout the company until someone is found. Collaborative technologies today allow you to easily search profiles within your company based on keywords or tags to allow you to find that person without having to ask anyone. Let's say you wanted to work on a strategy document with your team. The typical approach here has been for one person to get started on something, then to save it with their initials in the filename, and then send it off. From there any other edits are done by others who all add their own initials to the filename and keep sending it back and forth. Many dozens of emails can be sent by the time this is completed, resulting in a scattered mess of information that is hard to find, share, or collaborate on. Today, an employee can simply create a group dedicated to the project where employees can either collaboratively create the document online or where they can easily upload and comment on new versions. Everything is sorted, searchable, and organized.

There are hundreds of examples of how these new platforms are being used for things such as: employee onboarding, taking notes at meetings, staying on top of information, finding subject matter experts, getting access to information on the go, motivating employees and making work fun, brainstorming ideas and developing products, aligning an organization, and pretty much any other use case you can think of. The new technologies are finally enabling the behaviors we are used to in our personal lives to take shape inside of our companies, and they are doing so in a familiar way.

The key thing to remember with these new types of technologies is that for the first time employees are actually able to control the technologies instead of having the technologies control them. These technologies aren't just for large organizations either. My company, Chess Media Group, is by all accounts a small business and makes use of several collaborative platforms to stay connected and collaborative even though we are a virtual team.

In fact the new standard for measuring how enterprises class these new technologies is by looking at how consumer grade they are.

Although these platforms have been around for a few years now their level of sophistication is dramatically increasing. You may have heard of Watson, IBM's artificially intelligent supercomputer, which is now starting to become commercialized. Here we have a computer that is not only able to beat the world's best players at Jeopardy but it is also able to help doctors diagnose patients, answer and respond to customer service inquiries, and process legal documents to help legal professionals make decisions. Imagine being able to have this type of a virtual "smart" assistant in your workplace that can help you figure out projects to work on, answer questions for you, actually do some of the work for you, and assist you in your work life. Most people with an iPhone already have access to Siri. Now imagine having something like a more powerful and more intuitive Siri for the workplace.

Impact summary: Allows organizations to connect and engage people and information, anywhere, anytime, and on any device.

Big Data

By using the same earlier chess analogy we are now producing data that is increasing at an exponential rate. According to an IDC Digital Universe Study called "Extracting Value From Chaos,"[1] in 2011 more than 1.8 zettabytes of data was produced. This is the equivalent of every single person having 215 million high-definition MRI scans every single day. It's also the equivalent of building the Great Wall of China using 57.5 billion filled 32GB Apple iPads at twice the height of the original. Needless to say, this is a lot of data. This number is expected to reach almost 8 zettabytes by 2015 and 40 zettabytes by 2020.

Data is produced and created via almost any action we take today that "connects," whether it's making a phone call, sending a tweet, watching a Netflix movie, buying something on Amazon, browsing the web, playing a game online, or uploading a document. This amount of data can provide amazing amounts of information about a person, or more aptly, a potential or current employee.

Organizations can make use of all sorts of data when it comes to potential and existing employees. Today many organizations have a lot of data on their employees stored in HR systems, CRM applications, collaboration platforms, and any other piece of software they use to get work done. Combine that with public data such as Twitter conversations, topics covered on blog posts, employees who might be connected to Facebook, and LinkedIn contacts, and you have a lot of information about someone. The challenge is that for most organizations nothing is done with this data, it just sits around in multiple systems and can't be used to reveal any insights. Imagine how much we can know or figure out about someone when getting access to all of this information.

Data can be used to better understand what tasks or projects employees might be good at, predicting burnout or when an employee might be getting ready to quit, which employees should be promoted, or which potential employees might be the greatest assets to the company. In fact this concept of applying "big data" to the workplace is starting to be known as *people analytics*. Consider that most decisions and judgments about people within organizations are based on subjective information or data that might lie on the surface; things like GPA, what college people attended, how much money they brought into the company last year, the number of hours people work, how they dress, and other such easily available information. But companies like Knack are changing all of that.

Knack is a small but growing company based in Silicon Valley that makes games that help identify human potential. There is a lot of science that goes into the development of these games, which include titles such as Balloon Brigade or Wasabi Waiter. With the help of psychologists, neuroscientists, expert developers and programmers, and data scientists, Knack is able to figure out a lot about you based on how you play a game. They analyze hundreds of factors when you play the game, including how long it takes you take a move, if you take certain risks, what you focus on, and many other things. In fact, Knack measures things down to the millisecond and collects so much data about each player that they can recreate your game play just by looking at your behaviors. The concept is based on the idea of looking at the DNA of a person you know nothing about, in its purest form.

A team at Royal Dutch Shell called GameChanger focuses on identifying disruptive business ideas—not an easy task because it's hard to identify the most promising ideas. Hans Haringa,[2] the executive helping lead GameChanger, had the idea of using Knack to help identify those promising ideas. He had around 1,400 employees who had previously submitted ideas play some games from Knack to see if it could accurately predict which ideas from which people would go the farthest. Shell kept track of all the ideas and how far they were in being implemented. The top 10 percent of the idea generators as predicted by Knack were indeed those who'd gone farthest in the ideation process. Shell could have safely used Knack to help predict which people and ideas to "bet on."

However, games like Knack can also be used during the interview and recruiting process. Mark Howorth[3] is now the COO at Panavision but used to be a partner and senior director of global recruiting at Bain & Company, one of the leading management consulting firms in the world. Before Mark left Bain they were experimenting with Knack to help solve three problems. Mark identified these problems as type 1, type 2, and type 3 errors. Type 1 errors occurred when someone would be hired for a job only for the company to realize that the person isn't a good fit. Type 2 errors occurred when people were rejected who were actually a good fit. And type 3 errors, which happened when the company would grow more aggressively than their current talent pool allowed them to. In other words, instead of companies like Bain being able to go straight to top schools like Harvard they had to look at second tier schools or focus on looking at PhDs. The problem was that instead of being able to interview a few people from a school like Harvard many more people had to be interviewed from other places and there just weren't enough resources to do that, so they needed a shortcut to find top talent.

According to Mark, companies like Knack can help organizations move toward more diverse working environments by helping eliminate biases such as how someone might dress, how they speak, if they are young or old, or what gender they are. Having them play games and then looking at the data allows organizations to not only move beyond biases but to actually understand the potential candidate in a very deep way, thus truly being able to focus on the best potential person for the job. This practice is far from mainstream but it's certainly being looked at closely by many organizations around the world. Companies such as Knack are helping pave the way for using big data and people analytics in the workforce.

The amount of data that we continue to produce is growing and the challenge for organizations is how to tap into that data to make better decisions around work. People analytics is an interesting space to watch in the coming years.

Impact summary: More data means more potential information that can be gathered about anything. This can lead to better decision making. Being able to filter the information and make sense of it is crucial.

The Internet of Things

The *Internet of things* refers to the ability for devices to connect to a network and/or each other. Cars, refrigerators, desks, cameras, pants, credit cards, and everything and anything else you can think of will have the ability to connect to a device and a network to share information wirelessly. Today, the Internet is largely dependent on people to provide information, but what if devices could provide information independent of human contribution? The idea is that we could track, count, and analyze anything and everything we wanted.

Imagine your refrigerator knowing when you are out of milk and then it automatically reorders it for you. What if your clothing was telling you that you needed to lose weight or go exercise? Imagine your alarm clock telling your coffeemaker that you are about to wake up and that it should start brewing coffee. General Electric, Whirlpool, and Samsung already make and sell several "smart" appliances, which include washers, dryers, dishwashers, ovens, and refrigerators. These devices can all be accessed via an application on virtually any device so you can actually see and control what they are doing. As more devices become smart they will start to share more with each other and with you. One of the companies on the forefront of creating "smart homes" is Schneider Electric, which recently launched "Wiser Home." Once the system is installed in a home it can be used to manage energy ranging from controlling lamps and appliances to the thermostat or almost anything else. This can all be done whether you are inside the house or miles away from a mobile device.

Similarly, imagine you are on your way to work for a meeting and your car notifies your colleagues that you are going to be late because of traffic. With the Internet of things your company will know where everything is all the time. FedEx, the shipping and freight giant, is already enabling the Internet of things by using sensors to track packages, but it also looks at things such as temperature, humidity, and when the package was opened. In the workplace this means your devices "know" you better than you know yourself. Where you like to go lunch, when you have meetings, when you are most productive, who you work with, and who you should work with, when to leave and arrive to avoid a busy commute, and every other aspect of your workday will all be known, planned, and optimized based on the "things" that are communicating with each other.

All of these things are a part of the Internet of things. By 2020 analyst firm Gartner[4] predicts that there will be 26 billion units that have the potential to connect to each other and to the web, and this doesn't include PCs, tablets, or smart phones. Cisco predicts that the total number of connected devices will exceed 50 billion by 2020.

Some people immediately get a bit freaked out when hearing about this—it does sound a bit "big brother-ish." This concept is still at the very early stages for most organizations and there's still a lot we don't know about the impact that this will have on our lives (both professional and personal). However, this is still a trend worth mentioning as we certainly appear to be moving toward that direction.

Impact summary: The Internet of things is helping to create the vast amounts of big data. Devices will be able to "talk" to each other and to people on their own without human intervention or activation. This has the potential to make our lives and workplaces easier and more streamlined as well as help us to better understand ourselves, how we work, and how we live.

THE MILLENNIAL WORKFORCE

By the year 2020 millennials are expected to make up just over half of the entire U.S. workforce; by 2025 it's estimated that millennials will be around 70 percent to 75 percent of the U.S. workforce. Although the millennial workforce is clearly a different demographic it's not just the demographic itself that is significant.

This new workforce brings with it a new attitude about work, new expectations, a different set of values, and different approaches to how work should be done. This is a generation that is starting to greatly question the value of universities, is more concerned about sustainability, and has the ability to learn and teach at will. Sure, anyone can do this, but for millennials this is how they grew up, it's the standard and what they expect in the workplace.

These are people who grew up with social and collaborative technologies who don't know what it's like to get 200 emails a day, to sit in a cube from 9 to 6, to wear a suit and tie to work, or to sift through old technologies to find people and information. This is a group virtually attached to a mobile device that's always connected. I explore this in greater depth under "the future employee" section of the book.

Not having social and collaborative technologies inside of organizations is going to be the new foreign way to work. Millennials are used to sharing and connecting with each other. They live a more public and engaged life and they are going to expect these new technologies and approaches to be in place at any company they work with. This means it's crucial to make these investments if you are planning on trying to attract and retain top talent. Not only that but many workers are going to be retiring to make room for this new breed of millennial workers. Many older employees have been at companies for a long time and when they retire they are literally walking out of their company doors with years of experience, information, and knowledge that needs to be transferred over to new employees. Organizations are literally seeing information walk out the door.

Impact summary: A new generational workplace means new behaviors, approaches, attitudes, and expectations about work and the workplace.

MOBILITY

We've all heard the stats and the stories about how our smart phones and tablets today are more powerful than computers were a few years ago and this trend is only increasing. This means that many employees are able to access the same people and information from these mobile devices as they can from their laptops or desktops. More and more we see employees working "on the go" while sitting in cabs, waiting at airports, or while standing in line somewhere, and it's not uncommon today for many companies to have satellite offices that consist of just one or a few employees who work from coworking spots or home offices. Cisco, the multinational networking company that employs around 80,000 people worldwide classifies almost half of their employees as remote workers.

Today with the advances in technology around the way we work, employees can work from anywhere, anytime, and on any device. The technological framework is there but where many are struggling is around the strategic approach to empower this change. The notion of working 9 to 5 in a cubicle and commuting to an office is dead. All you need to get work done today is an Internet connection.

The statistics support that 91 percent of the people on earth own a mobile phone[5] and over 22 percent of people in the world own a smartphone,[6] with that number projected to go up dramatically in the next few years. Mobile phones are now becoming the standard for us to stay connected to each other and information with 50 percent of mobile phone users using their devices as their primary Internet source. Larger organizations with global employees are taking advantage of this but so are smaller organizations that are now able to form and function with virtual teams.

These trends around new behaviors, the shift to the cloud, new collaborative technologies, the millennial workforce, and mobility are dramatically impacting and changing what it means to work, to be a manager, to be an employee, or to work at a company. They are the cornerstones for what the future of work is going to look like. The impact will be felt by everyone and anyone who is either currently working or seeking to find work . . . and it's a good thing.

Impact summary: Allows employees to stay connected and working even when they are on the go. This helps make employee location independent.

GLOBALIZATION

The definitions of globalization vary quite a bit and there is much economic discussion around this all over the web. I'm not going to get into the details of globalization so hopefully you can forgive me for the oversimplification that I'm going to apply here. According to Wikipedia:

> Globalization (or globalisation) is the process of international integration arising from the interchange of world views, products, ideas, and other aspects of culture. Advances in transportation and telecommunications infrastructure, including the rise of the telegraph and its posterity the Internet, are major factors in globalization, generating further interdependence of economic and cultural activities.

To simplify, it's essentially the ability to do business around the world without boundaries. We see organizations spreading out all over the world creating offices anywhere from California to Queensland in New Zealand. Organizations have the ability to sell and market their products or services anywhere in the world and are no longer bound by transportation, cultural, talent acquisition, currency, or communication barriers. Even startups that have offices in one local area can easily open up another location anywhere in the world. More and more it's becoming harder to differentiate if someone lives in another city or on another continent. Technology is a large driver for making this possible and it's something affecting small and large organizations alike. My own company, Chess Media Group, although small, has offices in the Bay Area and in Vancouver and we are able to work with clients all over the world with ease. Where we are located is now irrelevant.

This ability for organizations to operate anywhere in the world is dramatically changing how people work.

Impact summary: Talent doesn't need to be local. Organizations large and small can be comprised of international teams. Organizations can also develop a presence in any part of the world and work without boundaries.

WHY IS IT DIFFERENT THIS TIME?

Change happens all the time, in fact the only constant that we can be sure of is change. The mechanization of textiles, the printing press, the assembly line, steam engine, the computer, and many other things have all changed the world and many other things will continue to change the world. There are three reasons why the changes we are seeing today are uniquely different: the speed of change has increased, the world is connected, and everything is being disrupted.

The Speed of Change

Around 1,000 years ago (or so the story goes), a mathematician and inventor by the name of Sissa created chess. When Sissa showed his invention to the ruler at the time he was so impressed that he allowed Sissa to name whatever he wanted as a reward. Sissa told the ruler that what he wanted was the following: to put a single grain of rice on the first square of a chess board, then to put two grains on the second square, four grains on the next square, then eight and so on, basically doubling the amount of rice for each subsequent square. The ruler thought about this for a while and agreed. In fact he was a bit insulted that Sissa would ask for something as insignificant as rice, after all he was the ruler of the land, he could have given him a palace! So the ruler tells his servants to figure out how much rice he will need to give to Sissa. Boy was he in for a surprise. It turns out that if you were to start with a single grain of rice on the first square of a chessboard and then double it until you got to the 64th and final square that you would end up with around 1,000 times the global production of rice in present day. That much rice would be a mountain larger than Mount Everest. So as the story goes, Sissa then became the new ruler of the land.

So what does this have to do with the future of work? Famed author, inventor, and director of engineering at Google, Ray Kurzweil, came up with the concept of the second half of the chessboard. This idea basically deals with the fact that once the grains of rice reach the second half of the chessboard the growth becomes exponential. Today, we are at the second half of the chessboard where changes are happening at a more rapid pace and the impacts of those changes are having a deeper more dramatic impact. In fact, many believe that on the technology front we are outpacing Moore's Law, which states that technological processing power will double every 18 months.

Technology really is creating substantial disruption. In an article published in the July 2008 issue of the *Harvard Business Review* titled, "Investing in the IT That Makes a Competitive Difference,"[7] Andrew McAfee and Erik Brynjolfsson, found two interesting things in IT industry companies. The first is that the spread between companies performing at the top 25th percentile and the bottom 75th percentile (what the authors refer to as the spread between winners and losers) was increasing. This also reflects the growing income disparity we see between individuals. In fact, the gap between the richest 1 percent and the rest of the United States is the widest it has been since 1920.

McAfee and Brynjolfsson also found that, "In turbulent markets, the top-selling company one year may not dominate the next. Today's 10th place company, for instance, might catapult to number one the following year."

In a conversation I had with *New York Times* bestselling author and Harvard professor Dr. John Kotter,[8] he addressed the fact that it's also the faster flow of information, money, products, innovation, and even people. His conclusion was that, "Your best practices won't save you." This means that if you can't keep up with the changes and the disruptions and your competitors can, then you are going to be in quite a bit of trouble.

For the previous historic innovations in history, businesses had the ability to be late adopters, and many of them in fact were. They waited to see what would happen before charting their course, many waited several years. When it comes to the future of work, "late adopter" is the same thing as "out of business."

Connecting the World

With the exception of the computer and the Internet all previous innovations were designed to connect and impact our physical world, after all, there was no virtual or digital environment. Then once the computer and the Internet came about we started to see this idea of connectivity spread. Connectivity is now making its way to everyone and into everything to build a truly connected world made up of people and devices; some say this is making the world a smaller place. In fact, over the next few years we can extend this to say that, "Anyone and anything that can be connected, will be connected." Thus far I have traveled to more than 30 countries, ranging from remote rice paddy villages in China and old cave cities in the Republic of Georgia to the remote deserts in Dubai and modern cities like Melbourne. Everyone, everywhere, is connected.

The rice paddy farmer in a Chinese province has the ability to access the same information and the same people that I do living in the Bay Area. That is fascinating.

Disrupting Everything

Never before have we seen a point in time where virtually every single industry was being disrupted. Everything from government and education to transportation and entertainment are changing, thanks to the connected world. We have new transportation systems powered by apps, artificially intelligent computer systems that are diagnosing patients, devices that allow people to accept credit card payments on their cell phones, governments opening up decision-making data to the public, cars being developed through crowdsourcing, wearable technologies that change how we interact with the physical and digital world, and 3-D printing, allowing virtually anyone to create and sell a product of their conception. It truly feels like a new world.

The disruption of every industry is also causing a bit of unrest as people struggle to define where they fit or if they will become obsolete. It's forcing us to adapt and change to stay relevant while giving rise to new business models, new products, new companies, new behaviors, and new ways of simply existing in today's world.

SHAPING WORK: PAST TO FUTURE

Since modern day organizations have first come into existence there has always been a flow of how work should be done; this flow typically went: organization, managers, and then employees. The "organization" in this case refers to C-level executives, stakeholders, and the corporate culture. Although organizations are comprised of people, the relationships, connections, and the vibe create a kind of "12th man" that also impacts how work gets done. Decisions were typically made at the top and held in place by the corporate culture. These decisions were passed

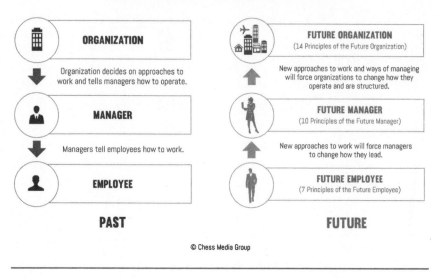

FIGURE 1.2   Shaping Work: Past and Future

down to managers who then passed them down to employees. This includes everything from how employees should dress, what time they should come into work, when they should get reviewed, who reports to who, and anything else you can think of. However this trend of guiding how work should be done is being completely reversed. Employees are bringing new approaches, attitudes, expectations, and ways of working into organizations. Managers must adapt to this new way of working by changing the way they lead, which then forces the organization as a whole to adapt to employees and managers. This shift can be seen in Figure 1.2.

The rest of this book talks about how employees are shaping the way work will get done and how managers and the organizations must adapt to the future of work.

CHAPTER 2

The Cog

Today's Employee

Let's get one thing straight right from the beginning. Employees are not incompetent idiots. They are fully capable, smart, intelligent, and creative people. So why do we treat them like the former and not like the latter?

The word and the concept of *employee* is fairly new to our lexicon and way of thinking, it was introduced less than 200 years ago around 1825 to 1835 and it hasn't changed since.

A DAY IN THE LIFE OF . . .

Meet Tara. She's an employee at a midsize company with a husband and two kids. Tara wakes up around 6 A.M. every day to help get the kids ready for school, but first she checks a few emails. She drops off the kids and then heads to work. After her 45-minute drive she arrives at 8:30 A.M.; by the time she gets situated her workday starts at around 9 A.M. She checks her email again and then goes into her first meeting. Then, she gets to work on a presentation she has been working on, a policy document, and a strategy document that she needs to provide her input on. She starts working and then her boss emails her asking her a question. She quickly responds and gets back to work putting a few more slides together. Then it's off to another meeting and then lunchtime. After lunch she checks her email again, works on her tasks a bit more, checks email again, and attends another meeting. It's 5 P.M. and she scrambles to head out of the office to make it home by 6 P.M. so that she can have time to go to the gym and have dinner with her family by 7:30. After dinner she checks her email again and works for another hour or so. Then she watches 30 minutes of TV and falls asleep, only to do that all over again the next day.

In this story Tara can be Greg, Christina, or anyone else. There are plenty of variations of this story but on average this is what the life of an employee looks like. It's frantic, hectic, stressful, repetitive, and has to fit neatly into a little box. The scary thing here is that employees have no say in what this day looks like. It's all dictated by the company they work for and the few people who "make the rules."

Reading through that story hopefully raises a few questions in your mind such as:

- Why can't Tara work from home some of the time?
- Why can't she just get to work later to avoid traffic and leave early as well? She can finish up whatever she needs to do at home.
- Why is she checking email so often?
- Why is her day so packed and hectic?

It probably also makes you think, "Wow, her work life doesn't sound that great but it sounds a lot like mine." This scenario is all too common not just for established employees but also for recent college graduates or employees just entering the workforce.

Imagine you just graduated with honors from a pretty good college with a double major in economics and psychology. With your excitement and passion you start looking for jobs and eventually land one working for a company in the L.A. area. The company promises to have you traveling with the business team, meeting with clients, and working on cool projects. Now imagine you're a few months into the job and have basically been spending the majority of your time making PowerPoint presentations and doing data entry while commuting an hour and a half each way, every day. Now imagine one day an executive walks out of his office and asks you to go get coffee for someone.

Shortly after this happened to me, I left. I was a cog, and I quit that job and never looked back. Working at this company made me miserable, depressed, and angry. Surely this isn't what work is really about, is it? I suppose I should be thankful for this experience because it has helped fuel my passion for all the things related to the future of work.

It doesn't feel good to be a cog. Sadly, this is how the majority of employees are viewed and have been viewed for many years.

THE TRADITIONAL IDEA OF AN EMPLOYEE

Employees used to be thought of as expendable and they didn't have a voice. They all came to work at around the same time, wearing similar clothing, doing similar tasks, and reporting to similar people. They worked in similar cubes, took lunch breaks at similar times, and worked in perpetual homogeneity, which is the quickest way to kill innovation. They did what they were told and didn't have the opportunity to engage with each other or build communities. Employees weren't encouraged or empowered to ask questions and no technologies were in place to allow employees to connect and engage with others. These employees were essentially supposed to work like robots.

In the past year or so there's been a lot of talk about how robots are taking jobs away from people, but the reality is that people have been doing jobs that were designed for robots to begin with. It's no wonder that many employees associate what they do with "drone-work," because it's perfect for a drone!

The big problem here is that many companies today were designed for robots and staffed by people. We have to change that around and focus on building companies for people. This is exactly what it sounds like—the idea that companies should be created and run by the people who work there and not automatons.

ENGAGEMENT IS IMPORTANT BUT LACKING

Employee engagement can be defined in many ways but regardless of where your company is or how big it is, having an engaged team is important. Gallup, an advisory and research firm, defines engagement by asking a series of 12 questions. The gist of an engaged employee is someone who cares about and enjoys the work that they are doing and feels connected to the people they work with and the company they work for. Many still believe that money is the best way to fuel engagement and motivation but in his book *Drive: The Surprising Truth About What Motivates Us*, Dan Pink points out that this is only true for mechanical and repetitive tasks. This was effective in the past because most companies were employing people to do just that. However, this is not the case today. Innovation and creativity are now required from employees and in this type of an environment money as an incentive can actually do more harm than good.

Today, the lack of employee empowerment in organizations is staggering. It's everywhere from the ticket agent at an airline gate who says, "I'm sorry the system doesn't let me do it," to the employee working for a large organization who needs to get two signatures to get approval to purchase a new $300 desk, to the social media manager who needs to get approval from her boss before she sends out a tweet on behalf of her company three days later. Meanwhile many organizations keep trying to throw money at the problem wondering why it's not doing anything. It's like trying to throw gas on a fire to put it out.

Thanks to technology, individuals have the ability to fund everyone from a farmer in Senegal on a platform like Kiva to a budding new entrepreneur creating a new technology in San Francisco on a platform like Indiegogo. We can buy cars, take out loans to buy houses, save for college funds, and plan international vacations. Yet for some reason we still need to get approval to buy pens at work. Gallup's recent 2013 report on "The State Of The Global Workplace"[1] found that only 13 percent of employees are engaged at work (defined as feeling a proud connection to their company), 63 percent are not engaged (defined as "checked out"), and 24 percent are actively disengaged (defined as acting out their unhappiness and undermining coworkers). Adding up the last two numbers, 87 percent of workers in the world are emotionally disconnected from their workplaces. Essentially this means that employees are sleepwalking through their jobs . . . a.k.a. they are zombies! For those of you who are secretly wishing that a zombie apocalypse would actually happen, let me tell you, it is right in front of our very eyes. Another report by Kelly Outsourcing and Consulting Group released in 2013, called "Employee Engagement and Retention,"[2] surveyed 120,000 people in 31 countries and found that 43 percent of employees frequently think about quitting their jobs. But again, looking back, this shouldn't come as that much of a surprise to us.

Think about how we describe work: We have the Monday morning blues; terrible Tuesday; hump day Wednesday; thirsty Thursday (where employees drink to cope with the week!); and then we are so overjoyed with thank goodness it's Friday!

Some may question the importance of employee engagement but research shows it has a dramatic impact on the bottom line. Gallup did research in 2012, which looked at almost 50,000 business or work units spanning 1.4 million employees around the world. Gallup further broke this down into groups of quartiles and found that compared with bottom-quartile units, top-quartile units experience things such as:

- 21 percent higher productivity
- 22 percent higher profitability
- 25 percent lower turnover (in high-turnover organizations)
- 10 percent higher customer metrics

Furthermore, in March of 2013 a meta-analysis of 58 independent studies was published in the *Journal of Applied Psychology* called, "Missing Link in the Service Profit Chain: A Meta-Analytic Review of the Antecedents, Consequences, and Moderators of Service Climate,"[3] the authors found a strong linkage between employee attitude and behaviors and customer satisfaction. In other words if your employees are unhappy and not engaged then the customer experience will be less satisfactory. The internal climate influences the external one. That alone should be powerful enough to get organizations to take engagement seriously.

All sorts of studies, numbers, and research reports can be thrown around but it's not necessary. Simply ask some people you know (or strangers) what they think about their job and have them give you honest feedback. I do this all the time at conferences and events.

It's not to mean that all jobs are bad, they aren't. In fact, after the recent economic tragedies many people are just happy to have any type of job at all. It's completely understandable that some people just want to make money to provide for their loved ones and themselves. Still, why shouldn't it be a realistic expectation to do this while enjoying the work you do for a company that you believe in?

There are many people in the world who enjoy what they do and like the companies they work for, that's great; but why aren't there more? Why aren't there more people who get excited to wake up in the morning to go to work? In fact, in a *New York Times* article from a few years ago published on March 14, 2006, titled, "The Claim: Heart Attacks Are More Common on Mondays,"[4] a study was referenced that showed that heart attacks happen most frequently on Monday as employees fear and stress out about returning to work.

Why is having a job that you like, that inspires and challenges you, and one where you are excited to go to work every day, the minority and not the majority? I suppose this shouldn't come as a surprise based on the preceding information, but it requires change.

In Figure 2.1, you can see one of the biggest reasons for such high levels of disengagement around the world; the gap that exists between how organizations approach work and the speed at which work is evolving.

In other words, practices, attitudes, values, strategies, technologies, and ways of working are evolving and changing at a rapid pace, whereas organizations remain stagnant. As this spread grows so does the rate

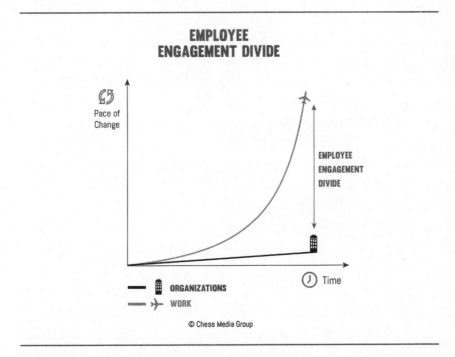

FIGURE 2.1   Employee Engagement Divide

of disengagement. This happens because employee expectations, needs, and wants are not met. As a result they become employees who just show up for a paycheck and don't really connect with the company they work with. To create an engaged workplace, organizations must adapt to the future of work.

THE FABULOUS FIVE

For the first time in the history of business we have five generations of employees who are working side-by-side, as seen in Figure 2.2. These are:

1. Traditionalists—Born before 1946
2. Boomers—Born between 1946 and 1964
3. Gen X—Born between 1965 and 1976

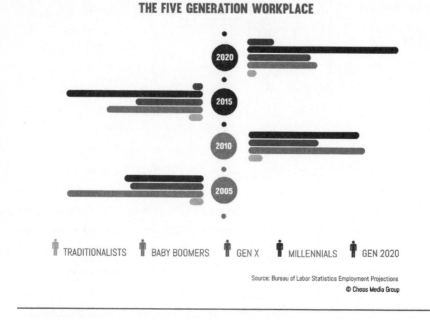

FIGURE 2.2   The Five-Generation Workplace
Source: Bureau of Labor Statistics Employment Projections.

4. Millennials—Born between 1977 and 1997
5. Generation Z—Born after 1997

Over the next few years the millennials and Generation Z (or Generation 2020) will become the vast majority of the workforce; in fact, by the year 2020 millennials are projected to be around 75 percent of the workforce. Here's a breakdown with data from the Bureau of Labor Statistics.

As can be expected, while the millennial and the Gen2020 generation increases in size the Gen Xers, baby boomers, and traditionalist workforce shrinks. However, this isn't just a change in demographics, along with this is also going to come a sweeping set of changes in how employees work, how managers lead, and how companies are structured and run; hence, the point of this book.

Consider this: When we first landed on the moon the average age of the NASA employee who was in that room making that happen was between 26 and 28 years old (depending on the source). When the Space Shuttle Atlantis left Earth on May 11, 2009, the average NASA civil servant's age was 47. The average age of a NASA new hire today is 41. According to a PwC report titled "State of the Workforce: PwC Saratoga's 2013/2014 US Human Capital Effectiveness Report,"[5] "63.3 percent of U.S. executives will be eligible to retire in the next 5 years and 33 percent are currently eligible to retire." Meanwhile, a 2013 report by EY (Ernst & Young) found that in the past five years: 87 percent of millennial workers took on management roles, versus 38 percent of Gen X and just 19 percent of boomers. To sum up, this basically means that the people who are running our organizations today are going to be leaving and will be replaced by workers with new ideas, new approaches, new strategies, and new ways of doing things and thinking about work, and this is going to happen at a rapid pace.

When it comes to the future of work there has been a lot of emphasis placed on millennials. Granted we are an important factor in shaping what the future of work looks like, millennials are but one of the five trends mentioned earlier. In other words, the future of work isn't just about millennials.

Millennials are going to be the majority workforce in the next few years but they aren't going to be the only employees in the workforce. So although it might be tempting to just associate millennials with the future employee, the reality is that there are still going to be millions of other employees from other generations around the world who are not millennials and we shouldn't forget about them. The future employee isn't just a younger employee it's an employee with new attitudes about work and new styles of working—regardless of whether they are 22 or 62.

It's also important to remember that before millennials, other generations such as baby boomers and Gen Xers were the majority of the workforce. When Generation Z becomes the majority workforce and starts relying on teleportation, self-driving cars, and artificially intelligent robots at work, then I and the rest of the millennials will have to adapt to that as well. Sports teams bring together players from different parts of the world, with different ages, backgrounds, values, and skills. Somehow they are able to learn how to play together. The same is true for the world of work. Any time groups of people are brought together they will have different ways and preferences of doing things. The world of work needs to evolve and although millennials aren't the only factor helping to shape that evolution they are a powerful force that is forcing organizations to adapt faster. Part of that is because of their sheer number. The transition to new ways of working, leading, and building organizations has already started.

CHAPTER **3**

Seven Principles of the Future Employee

When it comes to future employees there are seven unique principles that comprise the ways in which they are going to work and expect to work.

As you can see in Figure 3.1, future employees will:

- Have a flexible work environment where they can work anytime and anywhere.
- Be able to shape and define their own career paths instead of having them predefined for them.
- Share information internally in an open and transparent way in real time.
- Have the opportunity to become leaders without having to be managers.
- Collaborate and communicate in new ways.
- Shift from being knowledge workers to learning workers.
- Learn and teach at-will.

As the future employee brings these new attitudes and ways of working, managers and the organization will have to adapt. This is what the future employee looks like . . .

© Chess Media Group

FIGURE 3.1   Seven Principles of the Future Employee

Has a flexible work environment/connects to work.

Prime trends impacting flexible work: Behaviors shaped by social media technologies, globalization, technology, mobility, millennial workforce.

When most people think of flexible work they immediately think of two things: working anywhere and working anytime. However, flexible work actually has three components. The ability for employees to work anytime. The ability for employees to work anywhere. And, the overall focus on employee outputs not just on inputs. Although this third component is important; for the most part, when people talk about flexible work they are referring to the first two. Simply allowing employees to work from home while expecting them to be attached to their computers from 9 to 5 isn't considered flexible work, it's just working from home without the commute. Although this may be better than commuting to the office for many, it's still just a part of the way there.

THE THREE COMPONENTS OF FLEXIBLE WORK

As you will see, not every organization calls their programs "flexible work." The terminology is irrelevant and in fact many companies like to put their own spin and branding on it. However, what is common across the board is what these programs or initiatives are comprised of. For our purposes we will refer to this as "flexible work" which is comprised of three things.

Working Anytime

Fairly straightforward, working anytime refers to the employee's ability to work either at 3 A.M. or 3 P.M. There are exceptions to this. For example, some organizations allow employees to work anytime provided it's between the hours of 6 A.M. and 10 P.M. But for the most part employees have the ability to set their schedule.

Working Anywhere

Again, working anywhere is also self-explanatory. Employees can easily work from a home office, coworking spot, or a café, provided they have a reliable Internet connection.

Focusing on Outputs Not Inputs

This is the component that most people miss. Flexible work isn't just about working when and where you want—it's also about focusing on outputs (or outcomes) and not inputs. In other words, it's not just about the amount of time that employees work but what they produce and the quality of what they produce that matters. For example, let's say you had an employee who worked 10 hours a day, he would always be the first one to get to work and the last one to leave. Traditionally this would be the type of employee who would get rewarded and recognized because clearly everyone would see how many hours this brave soul is putting in every day. Now let's say you have another employee who shows up to the office maybe once a week. She produces excellent work but nobody actually sees her come in. This is the type of employee who will be immediately judged as a slacker who never comes into the office. That is because most organizations and managers today focus on the amount of time that employees appear to spend doing something and not on what they actually produce. This has to change. Just because employees are "putting in hours" doesn't mean anything. They could just as easily be coming in to work to play chess online, which is a game that could easily take several hours!

Unilever[1] has around 175,000 employees around the world and recently it was faced with an interesting challenge. The company wanted to double the size of the organization while cutting its environmental footprint in half. In other words, grow and waste less. Unilever's goal is to have 30 percent of its roles be location-independent by 2015. To accomplish this Unilever has created what it calls *Agile Working*, which allows employees to work anywhere and anytime provided they meet their goals and responsibilities. This has been the biggest work shift at the company in more than 20 years; but it recognizes that it must be done if it is to remain competitive going forward and achieve its goals. Unilever as an organization is moving toward truly flexible work.

Some organizations offer just one of the above components of flexible work, others offer two, and still others, offer three. The ideal scenario for most is to have all three components in place, but it requires gradual change, so let's not be too hard on those that just offer one or two of the above. They will get there.

FLEXIBILITY AS A WAY TO ATTRACT AND RETAIN TOP TALENT

Unfortunately, for most organizations it's still mandatory to work 9 to 5 from a corporate office. However, new technologies today are making it easy for employees to work anytime, anywhere, and on any device. In a recent study that my company Chess Media Group conducted in May of 2013 called, "The Future of Work: Reshaping the Workplace Today. Building for Tomorrow,"[2] we found that 90 percent of employees believe that an organization that offers flexible work environments is more attractive to prospective hires than one that doesn't, but that should hardly be shocking information.

Most people assume that flexible work is just something that millennials care about, but nothing could be farther from the truth! According to flexible staffing firm MomCorps[3] (who surveyed 1,100 working adults in July of 2013), 45 percent of working adults would be willing to take around a 9 percent pay cut to be able to have a more flexible work schedule. MomCorps also found that 73 percent of working adults look at flexibility as one of the most important factors when considering looking for a new job or deciding what company they should work for. This number has increased by over 10 percent since 2012.

There's no reason why employees should have to commute to work every day to sit in a cubicle. Employees now have the ability to work from anywhere and at any time as long as they have a reliable Internet connection. Employees are working from cafés, home offices, and coworking spots from all over the world, especially if these employees are part of a smaller organization that might not even have a corporate office.

In fact, the notion of the corporate office as we know it is dead—that is, having a single physical place of business where all employees have to come to work at a certain time and place.

The 2013 Regus Global Economic Indicator of 26,000 business managers across 90 countries revealed that 48 percent of them are now working remotely for at least half of their work week. This number seems a bit high based on what I have seen; however, it will only continue to increase. On March 5, 2013 the U.S. Census Bureau put out a press release,[4] in which they stated that 600,000 employees in the United States travel 90 minutes and 50 miles to work (each way) and 10.8 million employees travel an hour each way. This is the virtual equivalent of having a part-time job while sitting and driving in your car. I experienced this firsthand commuting around three hours every day. It was miserable.

It's no wonder that many organizations today are leveraging this idea of workplace flexibility as a key factor in the recruiting process to attract and keep top talent. Small organizations typically see this mentality of focusing on outputs as the standard for how work gets done. Unfortunately this tends to get lost as organizations grow in size and complexity.

Although workplace flexibility used to be thought of as a perk, for the future employee it's considered a must-have. A 2010 study by the Society for Human Resource Management called "Challenges Facing Organizations and HR in the Next 10 Years,"[5] found that 58 percent of human resource professionals cite flexibility as the most effective way to attract new talent. This is expected to keep growing. Imagine someone graduating college who has the choice between working for two similar companies. One offers a flexible workplace environment and the other doesn't, where would that college graduate want to work? Where would *you* want to work?

WHY ISN'T EVERYONE DOING IT IF IT'S SO GREAT?

Workplace flexibility will absolutely become the standard way to work and it will be demanded and expected by the future employee. Although this may not be something that every organization offers today we do see the interest and adoption of workplace flexibility growing rapidly.

The truth is that the only reason why employees are still working out of offices is because it's what their companies have always required, not because it's something that everyone enjoys or finds to be the most efficient and productive way of working. It's the same reason why we use email, not because it's the best or most efficient way to communicate or collaborate but because everyone uses it. Change is never easy.

In fact, numerous research reports show that employees who work from home are actually more productive. Not only that, but the companies who support flexibility are themselves able to save many millions of dollars. Productivity would increase by hundreds of billions of dollars. The quality of life for employees would also increase. Research published in 2011[6] from the Umea University in Sweden found that "couples in which one partner commutes for longer than 45 minutes are 40 percent likelier to divorce." The Gallup-Healthways Well-Being Index found that employees who have longer commutes have more recurring neck or back pain, higher cholesterol, experience more worry, and experience less enjoyment. In a separate article published on February 7, 2012 called, "Engaged Workers Immune to Stress from Long Commutes,"[7] Gallup stated that workers who are engaged at work don't experience more stress and worry from long commutes. I have yet to find any substantial data or research that suggests that flexible work environments have a negative impact.

Change is never easy and for many organizations it's much easier for them to leave things be instead of try to do something different, but as mentioned earlier in the book, the rate of change is increasing and it's no longer good enough to remain static.

SOME BENEFITS

According to Global Workplace Analytics,[8] a typical business would save approximately $11,000 per employee per year if that employee were allowed to work from home just half the time. The employees themselves would save between $2,000 and $7,000 per year (from costs such as gas) and the national savings would be more than $700 billion a year. Aetna, an organization with around 35,000 employees around the world, sees around half of its workforce working from home, which has saved it around $80 million in real estate costs annually and a voluntary turnover rate of those who work at home, which is around 2 to 3 percent (compared to the 8 percent industry average). Intel, which employs more than 100,000 people around the world, has more than 80 percent of its employees regularly working from home. TELUS, a telecommunications company based in Canada with around 40,000 employees, has a goal to have 70 percent of its entire workforce working either while on-the-go (mobile worker) or at home by 2015. Its reliance on collaborative technologies have reduced its travel costs by around half in the past two years. Rick Holgate, PhD, PMP, chief information officer for the Bureau of Alcohol, Tobacco, Firearms and Explosives cited a study by AOL[9] Government Mobile Technology of 300 federal managers, where half of them said that employees would gain an average of seven hours in productivity each week if they were enabled to work via mobile devices.

The list of companies supporting a flexible workplace is large and is showing no signs of slowing down.

WHAT ABOUT FACE-TO-FACE COMMUNICATION?

Many people argue for the importance of face-to-face communication and I agree—it is important. What is being suggested isn't an abolishment of all human contact. After all, we are social beings and it's hard to think of anything more depressing than employees sitting around their homes staring at faces on screens all the time.

In my last book, *The Collaborative Organization*, I referenced a study that was done by sociologist T. J. Allen, which found that once employees are approximately 200 feet away from each other, their chances of communicating and collaborating falls to zero; they might as well be all the way across town; and 200 feet isn't that far, we're talking just down the hall.

The recent string of companies that at one point announced a "no work from home" policy has also started some debate around this. These companies include HP, Yahoo!, Best Buy, and others. There are a few things to be said about this. The first is that there are still employees who are working from home at these companies. You should never believe everything that the media puts out there. The second is that I believe these to be temporary shifts. Based on the conversations I had with various employees at these organizations, when they first started allowing employees to work from home there was no strategy in place, there were no guidelines or rules, and there was no technology framework to make it happen. Things just started to get out of control. There were literally employees working from home who had entire side businesses they were working on. Once the foundation is properly established I strongly suspect that flexible work environments will once again be allowed.

The goal of having a flexible work environment means just that—an environment where employees choose where they want to work and when. It's about giving freedom and choice to the employees instead of mandating that they do something one way or the other. If certain in-person meetings are required and the team feels it's necessary then nobody is saying don't have them. However, working from a corporate office isn't the only way to get things done. Again, we turn to Schneider Electric[10], which understands this concept of flexibility and as a result has developed three individual mobility profiles for its employees: "Resident," which includes employees who are situated at the office for more than 65 percent of all working hours, "flexible," which includes employees who are situated at the office from 30 to 65 percent of all working hours, and "nomad," which includes employees who are situated at the offices for less than 30 percent of all working hours.

Many organizations are also redesigning their locations to be more modern and conducive to collaboration and communication. By creating these types of environments the reasoning is that employees will want to come to the office and when they do, they will be more productive and effective at their jobs. Amazon, for example, is proposing to introduce new offices that look like transparent biospheres, which are filled with natural sunlight and plant life. Samsung is proposing to create a new office that looks like a circular and transparent doughnut where employees can always see each other. The proposed new offices for these companies and others are truly unique architectures unlike anything the corporate world has seen. These offices will make for truly amazing work experiences when employees are there.

COWORKING

Coworking locations around the world are now also being used to meet flexible work environment needs. There are around 2,500 coworking locations around the world today, which is an increase of 350 percent over the past two years. Eighty-eight percent of these coworking locations expect to see higher revenues coming in, 53 percent of large locations are considering opening up another one, and more than 66 percent of existing locations are planning on expanding their current spaces. An article published by Inc on March 3, 2014 called, "Number of Coworking Spaces Has Skyrocketed in the U.S.,"[11] cited that from 2012 to 2013 coworking locations have increased by 83 percent in the U.S. while memberships increased by 117 percent. These numbers also don't include the many companies around the world that are allowing other individuals to rent out their extra office spaces as well, thus turning them into coworking locations. Unofficial coworking spots are also all over the place, most popularly at cafés.

They are convenient and provide for an ad hoc and convenient location for meeting or working and offer all of the amenities that you would expect to find in any type of office. One of the many popular benefits that employees enjoy at coworking locations is the ability to work side-by-side with people at other companies. Often this helps spur innovation, builds potentially valuable relationships, and makes for a pleasant change of scenery.

Future employees must be empowered and given the freedom to work in a way that makes them most productive, effective, and happy.

Does this mean that company offices are going to go away? Not entirely. Some organizations will utilize their offices as coworking spots, others will utilize the space in other ways such as creating large auditoriums for events, and yes, others will indeed be getting rid of their large and expensive offices and real-estate properties. Schneider Electric has recently embarked on a journey to transform its more traditional offices into more collaborative coworking spaces for employees. Schneider Electric has more than 1,300 offices around the world with more than 150,000 people, so its task of office transformation is gradual yet extensive. Its approach is based on four principles:

1. Promote collaborative space focused on ergonomics.
2. Establish common areas based on the well-being of employees and enhancing business performance.
3. Encourage activity-dependent movement across the workplace and a variety of space types.
4. Provide individuals offices only on a demonstrated needs basis.

THE END OF THE TRADITIONAL WORK SCHEDULE

There's also something to be said for working a set schedule. Unfortunately most of our lives don't really fit the 8-to-5 corporate work box. However, years ago the only way that a manager could know if employees were working was to physically see them sitting in a seat for a set amount of hours every day. I remember when I did telemarketing many years ago (yes, it was horrible) dozens of us were sitting around in little half cubicles with nothing but a phone and a computer screen. A manager would sit in the middle of the room and monitor everyone else. If that manager didn't see you picking up the phone and dialing they would come over to you and ask you why you weren't working. In many companies today it still feels like this.

Thanks to collaborative platforms, virtual work environments, messaging, and video conferencing, we have the ability to stay in touch and work anytime. You no longer have to be physically seen to be considered working. Why should employees have to wake up at 6 A.M. to frantically have to get to work by 8 A.M. and why should they have to leave at 5 P.M. to get stuck in rush-hour traffic? The new standard for measuring or evaluating employees should and will be based on outputs, not what they produce, not on how often they are seen.

There's no logical reason why employees can't work a few hours during the day then go to the gym or relax for a few hours and then work again when it is convenient for them. Most people don't produce their best work in an office from 9 to 5. We all have different ways we like to work and different times we like to work and being able to have that flexibility not only keeps us happier but it also helps us be more productive. The bottom line is that work is moving from rigid to being flexible, in every way.

Customized work.

Prime trends impacting customized work: Behaviors shaped by social technologies, millennial workforce, and technology.

We can customize a lot of things in our life. The music we listen to, the type of computer we buy, the food we order, the clothes we wear, and plenty of other things. Is it so unreasonable that we should be able to have some level of customization over the work that we do?

When you first start working for a company you usually start at the bottom of the "totem pole." This means that if you get your first job in sales that you start off as a sales coordinator, account executive, then perhaps a sales manager, senior sales manager, sales director, and so on, until you have climbed all the rungs of the ladder. Some people call this "paying your dues," which is a concept I find to be absolutely archaic and ridiculous today. Once you begin climbing that ladder it typically becomes the only career path you have and many people end up getting stuck in that role for the rest of their careers.

The idea of customizing work is one that I find to be particularly interesting and while some companies have been exploring the concepts it's still relatively novel for most. The whole idea behind customized work is to allow employees to un-pigeonhole themselves in their careers. It's about putting the career paths in the hands of employees.

The future employee will expect to be able to customize their work. But what does this actually mean and what does it look like?

There are three categories for customizing work. The first is customization based on voice, the second is customization based on self-organization, and the third is customization based on choice. All three involve sharing, which is an absolutely crucial component for the future employee.

Customization Based on Voice

One of the many fascinating things about social media platforms is the ability it gives people to have a voice. This is a powerful thing as we have seen in the Occupy movements, the Arab Spring, and even in presidential elections.

This notion of having a voice is just as important and powerful within organizations. Today, if you had something you wanted to share with your company how you would do it? Let's say you had an interesting idea, a piece of feedback, or a discovery that you made. Chances are you would send an email to a few people and then it would die right on the vine. That's because today in most companies employees have no voice.

Internal social networks and collaboration platforms afford employees a new and unique opportunity to be heard. Employees can share their ideas, post what they are working on, discover people and information, and connect and build communities. And they can do this at scale. This means that employees can participate in conversations and discussions that they are passionate about or are interested in, the same way they do on social media sites. When employees use these technologies and share, their peers and managers see what they are contributing to and what they care about. Employees build "weak ties" in their organization, which are essentially bridges to people and information within the company. This is what leads to opportunities to move around within the organization.

Let's take an example. Assume that you were hired at a company in the sales department, you're fine with working in sales but your true passion is around sustainability. Your organization leverages a collaboration environment where employees collaborate and communicate regularly. You participate in as many conversations as you can around sustainability, you join groups, start discussions, and share your ideas and opinions. As you do this you start to get recognized as one of the go-to guys around things related to sustainability. Other employees and managers in that department notice your passion and enthusiasm and give you the opportunity to pivot departments.

Without sharing and building these connections chances are you would have never been able to make that move. Nobody would have found out about your passion for sustainability and you would still be doing sales. To make this work two things are required. The first is a collaboration platform that employees use and the second is a manager with the right mind-set to be able to make this pivot happen.

Customization Based on Self-Organization

Not only are employees able to shape their career paths by sharing their voice but we are also seeing some very creative things happening around organizations, which are allowing employees to actually self-organize and select the projects that they want to work on. This is a very common approach seen in managerless companies, which are discussed later. In a sense, these organizations are turning into types of hybrid freelancer environments where employees can see what projects are available and select the ones they want to participate in (or create their own).

Treehouse is a company that does just that. With around 100 employees, Treehouse is an organization that makes it easier for people to learn how to design websites, build apps, and learn about technology through a unique web interface.

Not too long ago they made an interesting shift; they got rid of all their managers. They didn't fire them; they just decided that they were no longer going to have those types of roles. I explore the idea of the managerless organization a little bit later but obviously not having managers can create challenges. For example, how do employees know what to work on? Well, they pick!

The process at Treehouse[12] is fairly simple. An employee opens up his internal collaboration and project management tool called "flow" and proposes a project for the company to work on. Details of the project are included such as roles required, goals, focus area, and so on. Then it's up to the employee to recruit people for the project. When enough people join, the project can begin. Every employee at Treehouse has the ability to submit and create a new project or to join a project that someone else is working on. If a project doesn't get enough support it's "abandoned."

Employees at Treehouse completely customize their work by controlling what they work on. Naturally they pick projects that they find interesting, which makes for a much more engaging and productive workforce.

The CEO of Treehouse, Ryan Carson, wrote an excellent series around how his company made this transition and what it looked like. The company is still learning and adapting things as needed but so far it's going very well. The full series can be found on the Treehouse blog, I highly recommend you read it!

Customization Based on Choice

What if you could dynamically change your work preferences? For example, how many hours you can work a certain week, where you want to work, how often you want to travel, what projects you want to work, and anything else? Deloitte[13] has been doing some interesting things around this with its Mass Career Customization program, which allows employees to change their work preferences. Currently these changes are able to be made twice a year and it gives employees quite a bit of freedom based on employee choice. For example, Deloitte employees can customize how much time they want to spend traveling or if they want to make a lateral move within the organization. While this process is still evolving at Deloitte it's an interesting example of how work customization is being implemented.

Deloitte's reasoning behind doing this was to give employees multiple "paths to the top." It's a bit like a "choose your own adventure" game.

Certainly having a combination of these three is ideal but customization based on choice is perhaps the most difficult to implement as it requires quick changes and updates as well as a reasonable investment in custom technology to make this happen. However, organizations can experiment with doing something like this on a quarterly basis or semi-annual basis like Deloitte does.

There are various approaches around how work can be customized to meet the needs of employees and the employers. One thing is for sure, the ability for employees to customize work will become the standard. Perhaps we will even get to a point one day where customizing work is just as easy as ordering something from a menu or configuring a few options on a web-based platform that makes the changes immediate. Dynamic work customization will be something to watch out for.

Regardless of the type of work customization we are talking about, the new collaborative technologies that organizations are starting to use are powerful enablers to make this notion of customized work a reality. The role of managers and the organization as a whole is discussed in other sections of the book but customized work is beneficial for the employees and the employers. The ability for employees to shape and create their own career paths is going to be the standard. They are no longer climbing the corporate ladder, they are creating the ladder.

This is an extremely valuable proposition to current and new employees who want a way to shape their paths inside of organizations. There's no reason why employees who get hired in a particular area or industry need to stay in that area. Our interests, passions, and ideas are constantly changing and the ability to adapt our work to those changes is not only valuable but crucial.

One of the top reasons why employees change jobs is to focus on career growth. They want to improve their skills, learn new ones, and move into areas where those skills can be developed. Essentially many employees feel as though they have reached a dead end and there's nothing else left for them. Why not allow employees to do that within your organization instead of having them leave?

Organizations are always on the hunt to recruit and retain top talent but research shows that the cost of finding someone outside of the company can be almost two times as expensive as recruiting within. The data shows that hiring internally is cheaper, quicker, and that there's a better fit.

MODULAR WORK

Stemming from the freelancer economy (discussed later), the idea of modular work is to allow employees to select the projects they work on the same way they would if they were freelancers. Employees pick and choose the things that interest them instead of being told what to do and what projects to be a part of.

Valve is a $4 billion video game company that uses this model. In fact, Valve is one of the companies discussed in this book that doesn't actually have any managers. Valve has created well-known games such as Half-Life, Counter-Strike, Portal, Left 4 Dead, and its game platform "Steam."

Employees at Valve work in a unique way; they are free to move around and work on any of the company's projects that they might find interesting. However, this type of working model is clearly not for everyone. Former economist in residence Yanis Varoufakis, who is now a professor at the University of Athens and the University of Texas admitted, "It is a bit disconcerting for people who enter Valve, because there is no one there to tell them what to do." On many occasions people simply don't fit in not because they are not productive or good people, but because they just can't function very well in a boss-less environment.

However, Valve not only has a modular approach to work, it also doesn't have any managers, which is a common element in organizations that offer modular work. This concept certainly puts a lot of responsibility and trust in the hands of employees and in the hiring process. According to the Valve Handbook (which as of now is public online[14]):

> Deciding what to work on can be the hardest part of your job at Valve. This is because, as you've found out by now, you were not hired to fill a specific job description. You were hired to constantly be looking around for the most valuable work you could be doing. At the end of a project, you may end up well outside what you thought was your core area of expertise.

Shares information.

Prime trends impacting sharing information: Behaviors shaped by social technologies, technology, millennial workforce, mobility, and globalization.

The concept of sharing isn't new; in fact it's been a core part of traditional knowledge management for many years. Sharing was typically done via things like legacy technologies, email, and meetings. Unfortunately, this wasn't as effective as most thought it could or should be. Most employees have always been accustomed to hoarding their information. They wanted to keep their ideas and feedback to themselves so that they would get the credit and the recognition. This is especially true in organizations that fostered individual competitive work environments, such as virtually any financial institution.

Then social media platforms such as Facebook, Twitter, Yelp, LinkedIn, and others came around, which in our personal lives enabled us to share, collaborate, and communicate in an open, easy, and scalable way. Today, we share . . . a lot! A typical U.S. office worker produces around 1.8 million megabytes of data each year, which is around

5,000 megabytes a day; the equivalent of more than 4,200 pictures, around 300 songs, or more than 30,000 word documents a day.

Our behaviors were altered and organizations are trying to adapt by deploying similar social technologies in the workplace. Similarly, the future employee shares a lot of information. This information can come in many different forms ranging from documents and presentations to ideas, feelings, meeting notes, or what the employee is working on. Not only is the increase in sharing happening through traditional means but also largely on collaborative technologies that many companies around the world are starting to deploy.

There are several important benefits of sharing. For the employee who shares they feel a greater sense of engagement and empowerment knowing that their ideas, feedback, and information are being consumed and explored by peers and managers. It creates a greater sense of ownership around projects and also makes work easier and more effective since the lines for communication and collaboration are open.

For the company the same benefit of creating an engaged workplace is also true, but so is the added value of innovation. When employees share information this can translate into new product ideas, new service offerings, the identification of new opportunities, or even cost-cutting ideas (employee innovation is explored in more detail later in the book). Sharing is not only a new behavior that employees are starting to more frequently exhibit, it's a competitive advantage.

SHARING AND STACK RANKING

Stack ranking, better known as *rank and yank*, essentially grades employees on a bell curve and gets rid of everyone at the bottom of the curve. Microsoft was notorious for its "stack-ranking" system, which essentially forced employees to battle each other. In fact, higher performing individuals did whatever they could do to avoid working with people at the lower end of the curve in fear of having their own rankings jeopardized. You can imagine that in an environment where employees are constantly forced to go against each other that the motivation to share, collaborate, and communicate is quite low as is the trust. Microsoft employees were actually quoted as saying that this type or ranking system forced employees to backstab each other and created an unpleasant place to work.

This concept was first introduced in the 1980s by Jack Welch when he was running GE and is credited with helping the organization increase its earnings 28-fold between 1981 and 2001. Stack ranking has been often debated and many organizations have since changed the way they evaluate employees and substitute more open and collaborative approaches instead.

At the end of 2013 Microsoft[15] got rid of its stack-ranking system in favor of a more open, collaborative, and team-based approach. Ironically, Yahoo! changed to a stack-ranking system a few days after Microsoft abandoned it!

The idea of hoarding information and having employees compete against each other is dramatically starting to change and not just from a management practice perspective. Collaborative technologies are not only allowing for this sharing of information to take place but they also allow for information to be archived, searched, tagged, and easily retrieved at a later time. Not to mention that these new technologies are allowing employees to build more relationships and connections with each other, which results in more trust being developed among employees.

Employees who share information are the ones who will move up within organizations. These are the people who will get recognized by their peers and managers and these are the people who will build powerful networks within their organizations.

The key thing here is to not just share things for the sake of sharing them but to try to add value and context to conversations, discussions, topics, or themes. Sure, there will be plenty of non-work-related sharing happening as well but that's to be expected and it's a good thing. When people connect and share (regardless of what it is about) they build relationships, which builds trust. These relationships help spur innovation. The ability for employees to share helps make innovation everyone's job.

Not sharing and using collaborative technologies is going to do employees (and the organization) more harm than good!

Can become a leader.

Prime trends impacting "can become a leader": Behaviors shaped by social technologies, millennial workforce, and technology.

In the past, being a leader was synonymous with being an executive or even a manager. It was not possible to be one without being the other. The truth is that many managers weren't leaders and unfortunately many still aren't. Additionally, employees were not and are still not seen as leaders; they are seen as the ones who serve the leaders, but as you see in the next section, this is now completely reversed. Today we are at a unique point in the world of work where leadership is no longer something reserved for the appointed few who sit at the top of the corporate pyramid. Leaders are no longer appointed—they are created by building a following, and today, any employee has the ability to do this.

Creating leadership is commonly done in our personal lives through social channels such as Facebook, Twitter, Blogs, YouTube, and other platforms. Think of how many people you know or know about who have used these channels and others as a way to build thought leadership and expertise in a particular area.

In fact, this is exactly how I started and grew my business, Chess Media Group. I started blogging and sharing my consulting experience, which grew an audience, which led to other opportunities such as speaking, columns in publications, more clients, and my books. I wasn't "assigned" these things, I had to grow them from the ground up and I wouldn't have been able to do it without social platforms that enabled me to share my ideas with the world.

Employees within organizations have the exact same opportunity and ability inside of their organizations. Previously, a few employees within organizations may have been recognized for performance or for a contribution, but for the most part the employees are largely unknown and unheard of. They don't really have many opportunities to become leaders. Collaborative technologies within organizations are transforming that by allowing employees to communicate, collaborate, and share across the organization. They now have a voice and can be seen by their peers and managers.

The employees who are active in internal collaboration platforms are the ones who will become leaders within their organization. You cannot become a leader without having followers and the best way to get followers is to, you guessed it, share. Keep in mind that just because you share doesn't make you a leader, but it gives you the opportunity to become one if your peers and coworkers start to respect, understand, and follow you and the content you are creating.

This a big shift for the traditional model of what a leader is and it challenges the old power authority model that many executives and managers are so used to. Consider what Peter Drucker wrote in his 1973 book, *Management: Tasks, Responsibilities, Practices*. "The fact is that in modern society there is no other leadership group but managers. If the managers of our major institutions, and especially of business, do not take responsibility for the common good, no one else can or will."

Clearly this is no longer the case. Leadership is now up for grabs and employees can become leaders on anything ranging from tennis or racquetball to design practices or creative marketing tactics. It's up to the employee, it's their voice.

Leverages new ways of communicating and collaborating.

Prime trends impacting new ways of communicating and collaborating: Behaviors shaped by social media technologies, globalization, technology, mobility, and the millennial workforce.

Today, email is the default tool we use for just about everything. Recent reports suggest that we send over 100 billion business emails every day and by the end of 2017 this will increase to over 132 billion.[16] We also spend around four hours[17] every day simply dealing with email, that's half of our work day devoted to email. On average we send around 37 emails a day and receive 78, which brings the total to around 115.[18] However, many of us either get upwards of 200 emails a day or know of people who do, it's not that uncommon. To make matters worse employees check their email an average of 36 times an hour and it usually takes them around 16 minutes to refocus on a task after checking email.[19] We check email first thing when we wake up and it's the last thing we look at before we go to bed. Email rules our lives . . . or it used to, anyway.

The future employee doesn't rely on email for everything. In fact, email is a secondary form of communication and collaboration for the future employee. Instead, collaborative platforms are used, which are much more effective and efficient. Here employees can post updates on what they are working on, can easily have discussions, jump on video calls, store ideas, or collaboratively create a document, find people and information, and do just about anything else they need to get done without ever having to look inside of their inbox.

How we communicate and collaborate isn't just limited to email, though. Employees used to work on company-sanctioned computers, had to use company-issued phones and other technologies that the company mandated. Today, that is all going out the window. Employees are working on devices that are convenient for them. This could mean using their cell phone to make calls (instead of an existing telephony system), working on their personal Mac (instead of on their company-assigned PC), or working on documents via a collaboration platform (instead of email). Employees here are making the choices and organizations need to be prepared for that.

From knowledge worker to learning worker.

Prime trends impacting learning versus knowing: Millennial workforce, technology, mobility, and behaviors shaped by social technologies.

Knowing something used to be the standard commodity for moving up in the world. You had knowledge and experience and people wanted to hire you for that. I remember when I first graduated college I had a hard time finding a job because I didn't really have any relevant job experience and didn't "know" how to do everything I would be hired to do, but how was I supposed to get experience if nobody would hire me for my first job? It was a painful catch-22 because organizations today are focused on what you have done, not what you can do. During my job interviews I would tell the managers, "I may not know how to do everything but if you give me a few weeks I'll be doing whatever I need to do better than everyone else." That's because I knew how to learn and adapt what I learned into different settings and scenarios.

Much of what I do today around helping organizations understand the future of work didn't exist. None of the platforms we use today were in existence; there was no Facebook, Jive, Yammer, Twitter, or LinkedIn. There was no iPhone, iPad, Siri, Watson, or a bunch of other things that have so dramatically impacted our lives. We didn't have the same behaviors either. Many of us didn't share information openly and we didn't live such public lives. Yet somehow, here I am. Not because of what I knew or had experience doing but because of what I learned and was able to apply.

The world is changing so quickly that by the time new college students graduate, much of what they have learned is far less relevant and in many cases just obsolete. This means knowledge and experience are no longer the primary commodity.

Instead, what is far more valuable is to have the ability to learn and to apply those learnings into new and unique scenarios. It's no longer about what you know, it's about how you can learn and adapt.

On March 30, 2013 Thomas L. Friedman wrote a column for the *New York Times* called, "Need a Job? Invent It."[20] In that article Thomas interviewed Tony Wagner, author of, *Creating Innovators*, and a Harvard education specialist. Wagner said:

Today because knowledge is available on every Internet-connected device, what you know matters far less than what you can do with what you know. The capacity to innovate—the ability to solve problems creatively or bring new possibilities to life—and skills like critical thinking, communication and collaboration are far more important than academic knowledge. As one executive told me, "We can teach new hires the content, and we will have to because it continues to change, but we can't teach them how to think—to ask the right questions—and to take initiative."

THE DECLINING VALUE OF COLLEGES

The graduating class of 2013 is facing an average student debt loan of $35,200.[21] On average, students wanting to get an MBA had to take out a loan of $100,000 and the same is true for students graduating with a JD. This type of debt is forcing many to rethink the value of educational institutions. The future workforce is already learning and getting access to any type of information they want and need well before they enter a university. They already have the ability to find their passions, identify their strengths, and start businesses.

Consider the Massive Online Open Courses that are available today. These are online classes or courses that anyone can take on almost any subject and learn the same information that they would at a university for a fraction of the cost (or even for free). Sites like Udemy, Coursera, Udacity, and Khan University are just a few examples of places where anyone can get an either free or low-cost yet high-quality education on any topic ranging from Six Sigma to photography.

Education is becoming modular where students are taking courses they like instead of committing themselves to entire majors with a linear progression. For example, instead of committing to four economics degrees, many people are now taking courses on topics such as Power-Point, calculus, photography, marketing strategy, or anything else they have an interest in or desire to learn about.

According to a report released in January of 2013 by the Center for College Affordability and Productivity called, "Why Are Recent College

Graduates Underemployed,"[22] almost half (48 percent) of employed U.S. college graduates are in jobs that the Bureau of Labor Statistics (BLS) suggests require less than a four-year college education and 37 percent are in occupations requiring no more than a high school diploma. The authors of the report find that we have (and will continue to have) far more people with bachelor's degrees then we do jobs that require bachelor's degrees. In fact they propose two scenarios. Either college enrollments begin to fall or we will see what the authors jokingly refer to as people having a master's degree in janitorial studies.

Even though the perceived value of colleges may come into question, research from the Hamilton Project, a think tank on economic policy, released a report in mid-2013, which uncovered some interesting findings. The authors of the report are Michael Greenstone, a 3M professor of environmental economics at MIT, and Adam Looney, senior fellow at the Brookings Institution. They found that college graduates with a bachelor's degree would earn more than $500,000 more than an individual with just a high school diploma over their lifetime.

In their analysis the Hamilton Project also uncovered the returns on various types of education compared with other forms of investment. Investing in an associate's degree appears to yield the highest rate of return when considering the investment made. However, even attending some college and then dropping out yields a higher investment than stocks, gold, treasury bonds, T-bills, and housing, as shown in Figure 3.2.

According to Greenstone and Looney:

> The graph shows that, on average, attending some college but not receiving a degree also has a higher return than all other conventional investments. The annual rate of return of an investment in some college was 9.1 percent. This rate of return is more than 3 percentage points higher than the average stock market returns and 7 percentage points higher than the returns from investing in Treasury bonds.

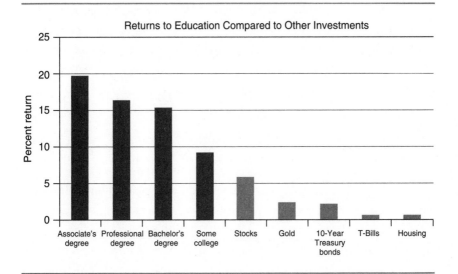

FIGURE 3.2   Returns to Education Compared to Other Investments

Note and sources: Sample is civilian, natural-born U.S. citizen population. Earnings data come from the Current Population Survey (2010–2012) and tuition data come from NCES (2012). An individual with some college was assumed to have stayed in college for 1.83 years, the average duration of postsecondary schooling of individuals reporting "some college." Data for returns to other assests come from Robert Shiller, the National Mining Association, and the Federal Reserve Bank of St. Louis and reflect real returns between 1928 and 2012.

Of course, the high rate of return associated with attending a few years of college does not imply that dropping out of college is a better option compared to completing a bachelor's or associate's degree. Graduates with a bachelor's degree annually make about $32,000 more than individuals with only some college. Instead, what this analysis suggests is that the downside risk of trying for a college degree but not making it all the way to a degree is not that bad, and could still be worth the investment of time and tuition.

The sad reality is that many organizations today simply use college degrees as a way to screen applicants. If you don't have a degree on your resume then your application is trashed. Many prospective students are now forced to ask themselves some tough questions:

- Is it worth it for me to pursue an advanced degree such as an MBA or JD or will I be better served working right away?
- Is getting a bachelor's degree even worth getting or should I teach myself the skills I want to learn and do my own thing?

On June 17, 2012 *Bloomberg* published an article called, "End U.S. Student Loans, Don't Make Them Cheaper."[23] In the article *Bloomberg* cited the Bureau of Labor Statistics stating that the United States has 115,000 janitors, 83,000 bartenders, 323,000 restaurant servers, and 80,000 heavy-duty truck drivers with bachelor's degrees. This number exceeds that of uniformed personnel in the U.S. Army.

I have a theory that the "zombification" of the workforce starts before employees even enter the workforce. It can start in universities. Although we see the future workforce prioritizing other things above salary, I believe that the greater the debt graduating students have, the higher the chance that they will take a job purely focused on money regardless of whether they actually care about the company they work for or the job that they will be doing.

When you consider the overwhelming amount of debt that many graduation students have, it's not hard to see this is a plausible theory.

Learning and teaching at will.

Prime trends impacting learning and teaching at will: Behaviors shaped by social technologies, technology, millennial workforce, mobility, and globalization.

My little brother Josh just turned 22. He's still in college but has a passion for film and photography. He has some of the top-of-the-line cameras, editing software, green screens, microphones, studio lights, monitors, and anything else needed to essentially have his own little movie studio. The equipment he owns is very expensive and takes a long time to learn how to use and yes he paid for everything himself. So how did Josh, a 22-year-old young man, learn how to use all of this equipment without having to get a four-year degree in film, which many people spend tens of thousands of dollars to get? Through YouTube, discussion forums, online communities, and other social channels. He started off with a basic camera and worked his way up until he started to get more projects. Josh also puts videos on YouTube educating others on things like configuring a camera balance stabilizer and shares product reviews and ideas. When he has a problem with something or has a question he immediately turns to his communities.

This is exactly how the future workforce is going to learn and teach. Imagine a bunch of these "Josh"s within your organization: Is the current way you train and onboard employees going to match with them? For many organizations the answer is no.

Educating and teaching employees isn't just the responsibility of HR or managers. The future employee within an organization will be able to learn from others and teach others on a variety of topics ranging from creating presentations to how to submit a corporate invoice. This is what it means to learn and teach at will.

As collaborative platforms connect our people and information an employee will easily be able to take out their smartphone, film a short clip on how to do something, and post it for the company to see. Similarly, an employee will just as easily be able to ask a question or seek help by tapping into the collective intelligence of peers. Information is becoming democratized and we already see employees turning to external sources such as Google all the time to find answers to questions that they need answers to. The future of work is about employees turning to each other and learning and teaching at will.

NEW CRUCIAL EMPLOYEE BEHAVIORS

Along with the new approaches to work, which are going to define the future employee, there is also a set of new qualities that are now becoming more crucial than ever before. It's up to employees to make sure that they can embrace these qualities as they will be required to succeed and thrive in the new workplace. A lot of responsibility rests on the shoulders of the future employee and again these are crucial behaviors to have regardless of how big or small your organization might be.

I should point out that qualities such as integrity, trust, and commitment have always been important and still are, but I'm specifically talking about qualities that are uniquely important to the future employee, which may not have been in the past. You may be able to identify several other unique behaviors that will be relevant to your workforce as well.

Self-Direction and Autonomy

If flexible work environments are to become the standard, then employees need to be self-directed to get things done. In other words, the importance of employee accountability has never been more important. There will no longer be a manager staring over their shoulder making sure that they are "working." Instead it will be up to employees to make sure they can stay on top of relevant tasks, complete things on time, and produce quality products and services. This is the responsibility of the employees if they wish to entertain the freedom and benefits of flexible work. A part of this is going to depend on clearly defining what the employee outputs need to be and when they need to be done. It's up to the employees to make sure that the quality of work they produce is high and on time. This doesn't mean that employees are meant to feel as though they are working on remote islands away from everyone else. Connection (both physical and virtual) is still available.

Filter and Focus

Today we are already pulled in many directions. It's not rare to see someone in a meeting who is checking email and working on a document while instant messaging with a colleague all at the same time. With the rapid increase in technology deployments comes the ease of being always connected. This means more information and more interactions coming in the direction of the employees. Employees must learn to filter the important pieces of information that come their way while focusing on the things that they need to get done. Just because they are always connected doesn't mean they always need to be available. We can expect that collaboration and connection will help breed super multitaskers, but again the key quality here is being able to know what information and people are relevant and what needs to be prioritized—in a sense, employees are their own project managers.

Embrace Change

For new employees and existing employees they must be comfortable with embracing change. Not just from a technological standpoint but from a behavioral one. Change can come in many forms whether it's a new management practice that seeks to abolish semi-annual employee reviews, or a new collaboration technology that relies on employees sharing information to succeed. Whatever the change is, employees must be able to embrace it and adapt to it instead of trying to fight it.

Amazing Communication Skills

It's true, communication skills have always been an important factor for employees, but it is becoming an absolutely essential behavior today, especially in the face of virtual and flexible work environments. Communicating ideas and feedback via a written status update on a collaboration platform or a video call are becoming the standard. More people will be seeing and interacting with the content that we create, which means that communications must be clear, succinct, and easy to understand.

Although the previous employee behaviors may be crucial, the goal is to get you to ask yourself, "What are the behaviors that I as an employee believe to be crucial?" or if you're a manager, "What are the crucial employee behaviors that we as a company must adapt to?"

Learning to Learn

Adaptation is based on the premise that you can learn. If you can't learn then you can't adapt. This means that for employees to succeed in the new world of work they must be able to learn new things and apply those things to the work they do. Thankfully it's never been easier to learn anything than it is today. Employees who turn a blind eye to change and those who aren't willing to learn how to teach themselves and find the information they need to get their jobs done are going to have a hard time.

SUPPORT THE FUTURE EMPLOYEE

The future employee isn't an idea or a concept, it's a reality that all organizations must be ready to adapt. In this section the goal is to paint a picture of what the future employee will look like and how they will work. The principles of the future employee are:

- Flexible work.
- Customized work.
- Sharing information.
- Becoming a leader.
- Leverages new ways of communicating and collaborating.
- Learning versus knowing.
- Learning and teaching at will.

However, these principles cannot just come to be, there are three supporting factors that need to be considered and addressed.

Management Mind-Set

Whether we are talking about flexible work, email, or customized work, none of the things outlined for the future employee will be possible without a different way of thinking about management. This is why the entire next section of this book is devoted to exploring future managers and how they must adapt. The traditional ideas of the corporate ladder, working from the office, and dictating work must be abandoned and replaced by new progressive ways of thinking about work (those discussed earlier). New behaviors are also required; for example, managers understanding how to use collaboration platforms to "listen" to employees who show a strong passion or interest for a particular topic or area, serving employees instead of the employees serving managers, and challenging conventional ideas and models of management. How new managers with new approaches will enter organizations is discussed in greater detail later but it starts with simply asking, "why." Why are reviews done once a year? Why do employees have to work 9 to 5? Why can't managers be more open and transparent with employees? Why does the organization have to follow a strict hierarchy? Asking the "why" will inevitably lead managers and employees to figure out the "how."

Regardless of how much employees push for things such as flexible work, in most organizations the managers need to grasp that concept, the benefits, and why it makes sense. This includes not just mid-level managers but CEOs. This shift in thinking will happen one way or the other as the new workforce begins rapidly entering employment over the next few years. But managers today have a unique opportunity to help lead this change and propel their organizations into the future of work.

Technology

Technology itself is never a solution but it is a powerful enabler. A car is useless if nobody drives it, a computer is pointless if nobody turns it on, and the Internet has no meaning if nobody connects to it. Technology is just a tool to allow and unlock behaviors and potential. Much of what was discussed earlier cannot happen without the use of technology, which should be thought of as the central nervous system of the organization. Technology is what enables sharing, flexible work, and democratized learning within organizations. The great thing is that today technology has never been easier to access and deploy. Collaboration platforms, instant messaging applications, and videoconferencing solutions are all based in the cloud allowing employees to stay engaged and connected to each other and information, anywhere, anytime, and on any device.

Laying the Foundation

When building a house you don't typically start from the roof and work downward. You start at the core on which the rest of the house will be built on top. The same thing is true for the future of work. Laying the foundation includes things like creating a culture of sharing and collaboration instead of one of individual competition (think Microsoft) and providing guidelines and policies for flexible work. For example, organizations need to consider if they want to cover the costs of coworking arrangements or if there is an expectation for employees to be online a certain time during the day (i.e., you can work anytime you want but from 10 A.M. until 11 A.M. please be online so that we can have regular interactions).

This also includes education and training. Employees and managers alike need to actually understand what the future of work looks like, how it impacts them, and how the company is going to get there. Helping employees understand this is perhaps the most crucial support mechanism for the future. One way this can be done is by developing councils, teams, or groups specifically devoted to exploring the future of work. These teams can find the research, test the ideas, and work with the rest of the organization to make changes. A great example of an organization that has "set the foundation" can be seen with Whirlpool.

Whirlpool[24] is the world's largest home appliance maker with more than 70,000 employees around the world. For Whirlpool, the future of work is a crucial investment. In 2013 the company introduced the concept of the Winning Workplace, which connects three major components: winning tools, winning environment, and winning culture. Lynanne Kunkel, their vice president of Global Talent Development, describes the approach for creating a Winning Workplace as "integrated" and "intentional." In other words, it's front and center, corporate-wide, and extends from the CEO to all employees. It's not a pilot program or a test, it's a more efficient, effective way of working to achieve the global business strategy. The objective is to empower, enable, and inspire employees to deliver results beyond expectations for consumers and Whirlpool. Winning tools include providing the necessary technologies that Whirlpool employees need to get work done with speed and efficiency. A winning environment means creating both physical and virtual places that encourage open collaboration, communication, and fast decision making. It's also about empowering employees to work when and where they need to in order to be most effective in achieving greater results. Finally, winning culture includes the core values, policies, programs, training, and education that shape the behaviors necessary to build and sustain the Winning Workplace. The extent to which Whirlpool has thought about the future of work demonstrates its clear understanding of what it means to create a foundation.

If your organization is to succeed and remain competitive then it must pay attention to how employees of the future are going to work and adapt. However, not everyone might be an employee in the traditional sense.

EXISTING EMPLOYEES

There is no perfect manual for dealing with office relationships. However, many readers may be thinking, "With all of the new employees entering the workforce what does this mean for the millions of employees who are already in the workforce?" The first thing that needs to be done is to eliminate any type of stereotypes that might exist. Not all younger workers are fluent with technology and are super multitaskers, and not all older workers are naive when it comes to new technologies. The reality is that there is a lot that multiple generations of employees can learn from each other. Although younger workers may be more fluent when it comes to new technologies, older workers may be much wiser when it comes to interpersonal relationships within the workplace. Younger workers might be better multitaskers, but older workers might be more detailed and organized. However, this is not specific to generations. Any time you have groups of people there will always be differences in opinions, values, and how they want to work. The best thing to do is to encourage open communication about any differences that might exist while providing plenty of opportunities for education and training around new ways of working. Employees, regardless of their seniority level, age, job, or function need to feel as though they can openly share how they are feeling about the way work gets done. Employees need to be able to connect and engage with each other. The same is true when assembling a sports team. Players play the game in their own way but through coaching, collaboration, and communication they learn to adapt to one another and play the game well.

In this case, the future employees are the ones leading the charge and while it should be recognized that their new attitudes and work styles will eventually become dominant, the change and process will be gradual. However, the way managers change the way they lead and the way the organization structures itself will play a large role in getting everyone on the same page. Later sections on the future manager and the future organization take this into account and focus on providing an environment where employees are empowered to make decisions and support each other.

EVOLUTION OF THE EMPLOYEE

This chapter covers many terms of how employees are changing the way they work and expect to work in the future. These changes are creating an evolution of the employee and Figure 3.3 summarizes this evolution by comparing the ways in which employees used to work in the past with the way employees are going to work in the future.

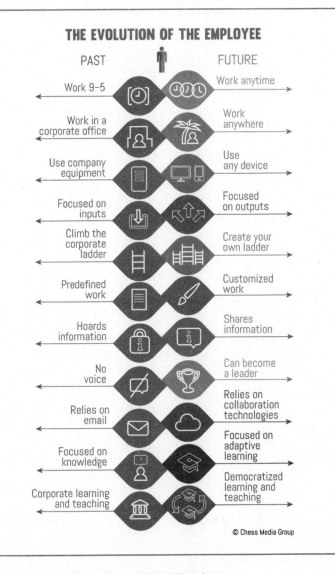

FIGURE 3.3 The Evolution of the Employee

CHAPTER 4

The Freelancer Economy

When writing this book I was debating on whether to discuss freelancers or those who technically aren't considered true "employees." However, this is such a big part of what's happening today and will happen in the future, that it simply cannot be ignored. There is a massive shift happening in the world of work that goes beyond what we think of as the traditional employee. In fact, an entire book can be written about this topic (perhaps an idea for my next book!), but I'd at least like to touch on it here.

According to Wikipedia, the term *freelancer* was first used almost 200 years ago by novelist and poet Sir Walter Scott to describe medieval mercenary warriors in his historical novel *Invahoe*. They were freelancers because they were not sworn to any particular lord and they were available to be hired.

According to a report by Intuit called the "Intuit 2020 Report: Twenty Trends That Will Shape The Next Decade,"[1] which was published in 2010, by 2020 around 40 percent of the U.S. workforce will be working as freelancers, temp workers, or contractors (some predict this number to get as high as 50 percent). This amounts to around 60 million people in the United States alone. A report by MBO Partners called "The State of Independence in America,"[2] which was released in September of 2013, found that there were around 18 million independents in the workforce in 2013. The demographics of this group is also quite diverse with one in five being millennials, 36 percent being Gen X, 33 percent boomers, and 11 percent matures (68-plus). According to a report released on January 2, 2014 by *Staffing Industry Analyst* called "'Online Staffing' Platform Businesses—Industry Segment Forecast Through 2020,"[3] the total global market predictions for this industry range from $16 billion to $46 billion in 2020.

Platforms such as Elance-oDesk (which used to be two separate companies that have just merged) and Freelancer.com are leading the way for creating marketplaces where people can get work and find jobs without ever leaving their homes. When the companies were separate oDesk alone did more than $1 billion worth of work to date and on Elance the number was more than $500 million. These two platforms which merged alone represent freelancers who work in nearly every single country in the world. Combined, they have more than 8 million freelancers and more than 2 million businesses working with them. Since 2001 Freelancer.com reports that the value of the projects which have been posted on their platform are right around $1.5 billion with around 11 million verified users.

Although many of the freelancers are still working at regular jobs, recent data from Elance-oDesk suggests that 72 percent of them want to quit to work independently full time and 61 percent plan to do so within the next two years. This can potentially lead to a mass employee exodus from traditional workplaces. By 2018 Staffing Industry Analysts expect the online work industry to reach $5 billion annually.

The numbers just keep piling up to support this trend. A recent report by Tower Lane published in 2013 called, "Surveying the New World of Work"[4] found that more than 60 percent of companies in the United States plan to hire freelancers in the next year. Naturally this also puts pressure on freelance websites to help make sure that companies can find freelancers that are a good fit.

Since modern corporations have first come into existence, we have become content with the idea that an employee works for one company at a time. The overall tenure of employees might have gone down, but for the most part the idea of working for one organization remained. It appears as though this very foundational idea may be in jeopardy as a result of the freelancer or what some call the *free agent economy*. What if "employees" worked for multiple organizations at a time instead of just one? Millions are already doing this, but it's definitely not the standard way of work, at least not yet. However, it certainly appears as though things may go down that road.

So What Exactly Is the Freelancer Economy?

This so-called freelancer economy is about people being able to leverage their skills and expertise to find work without having to seek full-time employment at a single company. It's also about the ability of organizations to tap into this group of people to get work done.

Anyone with knowledge or expertise in something can offer those services up for the world to see and use. This isn't just about younger people either. Many people who have retired from "traditional jobs" also leverage the freelancer economy to keep working on projects that interest them.

Most of the projects are done in a virtual environment and include services such as search engine optimization, marketing and PR, content creation, web development, or virtual assistant tasks. It's a completely virtual setup with an entire global marketplace behind it. Think of it as a type of dating site for business, complete with reviews, feedback, examples of previous work, skill assessments, and everything else you could want or would hope to know about someone before hiring them.

WHY IS IT POPULAR?

There are several reasons why this freelancer economy is becoming increasingly popular. As addressed earlier, many employees are not engaged in their jobs, yet they still possess skills and services that they can offer. The rationale for many people is, "Why should I work at a company, doing a job that I'm not that fond of, when I can easily go out and do my own thing and make money as a freelancer?" This is the exact mentality I had when I first went off on my own. I worked for an agency in San Francisco at the time providing online marketing strategy for their largest accounts. I won a pass to go to a conference during the week and wasn't allowed to attend despite being willing to work evenings and weekends to make up the work (which didn't have an immediate deadline). After I was denied I started thinking, "If I can provide value to these large organizations through an agency, maybe I can do the same thing on my own." That was the last time I worked for anyone else.

There are a few things that make freelancing very attractive.

Good Wages

Consider that the average hourly rate on Elance (when it was a separate entity) was $28 an hour, which equates to roughly $56,000 per year assuming that the person can work 40 hours a week.[5] On oDesk (when it was a separate entity) the numbers were similar and ranged from $20 to $40 per hour for technical work and $10 to $30 for nontechnical work:[6] however, these numbers have gone up around 30 percent since 2009, so there is a trend in growing wages for freelancers. In fact, MBO Partners found that 50 percent of Gen X independents say they can make more money on their own versus working for someone else. In some markets the demand for freelancers is growing quite rapidly. A recent article published by *Fortune* magazine on April 9, 2014 called, "Freelancer Pay Jumps, in Search of Quality Work,"[7] noted that many companies are willing to pay a premium for freelancers in less saturated markets. For example those with technical skills such as development, project management, and mobile or big data applications; even writers noticed a big bump. According to the article, this trend is going to continue.

In many cases these are higher wages than most entry level positions that someone can find, which usually start somewhere around $40,000 a year or close to $20 per hour. There are also plenty of people who charge much higher rates for their services, going up to $50, $75, $150, or even more per hour (even though they probably don't work full time).

Flexibility and Freedom

These are people who can earn a decent living while working on projects that they want, when they want, and how they want. They have complete autonomy and control over how they work and many even do so while traveling. It's akin to having their own business where they are the CEO. Freelancers usually have a good sense of how much money they need to make and can work required hours accordingly; it's the ultimate form of customizing work, which is an attractive proposition. This type of model fits everyone from the single freelancer who wants to work and travel to the person who has a family and works at home.

COMPANIES USING FREELANCERS

Many companies around the world are also starting to work with freelancers instead of hiring full-time employees. Unilever, NBC, Mozilla, and Panasonic are just some of the companies that are tapping into freelancers; there are many companies doing this, although a good majority of them are trying to keep it a secret. My company, Chess Media Group, also works with freelancers around the world when we need help on projects. For a small organization it's especially powerful to be able to quickly get quality help when it is needed. The value and the benefit here flow both ways.

Ad Hoc Teams

Organizations have the ability to quickly put together ad hoc teams to work on anything from creative art to marketing and PR. Let's say you have something that needs to get done right away or something that needs to get done but nobody to do it. Leveraging sites such as

Elance-oDesk allows you to fill those gaps quickly, easily, and at relatively low cost. In fact, according to the Tower Lane report mentioned earlier, 75 percent of companies that participated in their survey said they use freelancers because they need access to different skills at different times.

Testing

Many companies leveraging these sites have the ability to quickly test out various freelancers to see who they want to work with. Let's say for example that you want to hire someone to write a press release for you. You can give the job to three freelancers to see who does the best job, then you can hire that person on a more regular basis, all for relatively low cost.

Low Cost

The cost of hiring through these freelancer marketplaces is usually quite a bit cheaper than hiring a full-time employee. Even if the hourly rate is higher there are usually no ongoing overhead costs that need to be covered. You just pay for what you need and nothing more—it's an efficient system.

Global Talent Pool

One of the most appealing things about the freelancer economy is the ability for organizations to dramatically increase their talent pool. Virtual and flexible teams are becoming quite normal nowadays which means that potential team members no longer need to be located within a few miles of a company office. Organizations are now able to tap into the best and most talented employees around the world regardless if they are in the same city or on another continent.

More and more employees are seeking ways to leverage their skills and expertise outside of their current employment; these employees are also able to work on projects that they care about or are interested in and they can do the work when they want and where they want.

The idea of the freelancer economy challenges the very idea of what it means to be an employee and forces us to ask, "Will everyone be a freelancer in the future?" Is it possible that instead of employees working for a single company they will instead work for multiple companies doing a diverse set of projects at the same time? Or perhaps temporary workers will become the standard where employees will work for a single employer a few weeks or months at a time before going elsewhere? All of these scenarios are interesting to consider.

I think we will see a combination of all of the above. It's hard to imagine employees going away altogether and everyone being a freelancer. Many issues could potentially arise, such as working with competing companies, legal and cross-border issues, cultural challenges, the ability for everyone to make a fair living, and a host of other things. It's not to say that these issues cannot be resolved. Although this area is growing, I don't see becoming a freelancer as the standard way for everyone to work in the near future.

However, I do think that more people will continue to become freelancers while they are employed full time and once they are able to make a desired income will eventually transition. But, keep in mind that this transition isn't going to happen for everyone. There are plenty of people out there who work as freelancers who aren't making what they would consider to be enough to survive on their freelance wages full time.

What seems to be quite a realistic scenario for the future of work is that organizations will adapt to the freelancer model not just by hiring freelancers but by building their own environments focused on tasks and projects instead of long-term careers. This means that as an "employee" for an organization you will act just like a freelancer would—meaning that you will find the projects you are interested in and then once those are completed you will move onto the next one. This means that organizations will see much more of a combination between dynamic and static roles. The tenure of employees is already shrinking and the idea of permanent employees or careers will become arcane. Future employees won't be picking a career or a company to work for; they will pick projects that they want to be a part of for multiple companies around the world.

CHAPTER **5**

The Zookeeper

Today's Manager

I need you to be clever, Bean. I need you to think of solutions to problems we haven't seen yet. I want you to try things that no one has ever tried because they're absolutely stupid.

—Ender Wiggin, *Ender's Game* by Orson Scott Card

MANAGER OF THE PAST/TODAY

Now that we have a picture of what employees of the future look like and how they will work, the next step is to understand what future managers are going to look like and how they need to adapt their approaches and leadership practices.

Frederick Winslow Taylor was a mechanical engineer who is credited as being the father of scientific management, a concept designed to improve labor productivity and operational efficiency by analyzing work. His original idea focused on having more managerial control over workers, which meant more managers. Although Taylor died in 1950 it's hard to look around today's corporate world and not see many of his ideas in action today. Take, for example, the role of the manager as someone who should control and enforce.

According to Taylor (*Taylor, Principles of Scientific Management*, cited by Montgomery 1989, 229):

It is only through enforced standardization of methods, enforced adoption of the best implements and working conditions, and enforced cooperation that this faster work can be assured. And the duty of enforcing the adoption of standards and enforcing this cooperation rests with management alone.

Now, although the concept of scientific management has been thought to be irrelevant since the 1930s, we can easily see how some of this standardization and managerial control still persists today.

When speaking in front of a congressional committee Taylor also said (Montgomery 1989, 251):

I can say, without the slightest hesitation, that the science of handling pig-iron is so great that the man who is . . . physically able to handle pig-iron (product of smelting core with a high carbon fuel) and is sufficiently phlegmatic and stupid to choose this for his occupation is rarely able to comprehend the science of handling pig-iron.

The notion here was to assume that workers or employees were just supposed to do what they were told, that they weren't capable of really understanding any more than just the simple specific tasks they were told to do. Again, we still see this type of mentality in many corporations around the world where managers have access to and control all the information and just delegate tasks to employees.

The idea here isn't to point out flaws, or to deride Taylor or the many other brilliant management thinkers and leaders who came before and after him. It's simply to point out that what worked in the past doesn't necessarily work now. If you recall the analogy of the second half of the chessboard, things are now moving at a rapid pace, which means our organizations need to adapt.

Not all management practices developed in the past are bad or outdated, though. There are also plenty of theories and management approaches that were developed years ago, which are indeed still relevant today but need to be executed differently. Take, for example, the brilliant work of Douglas McGregor and his Theory X and Theory Y model from 1960, which is based on Maslow's *Hierarchy of Needs*. McGregor developed two theories for the role of management.

Theory X states that the role of management is to enforce control and coerce employees into getting their jobs done. It assumes that people prioritize job security (which we already see was no longer the case), that they inherently dislike their jobs, and that employees will avoid working when they can.

Theory Y states that employees may be ambitious, self-driven, and determined, and that work is just as natural as play or rest. It asserts that people have potential and the ability for creative problem solving and that decision making should be distributed and not just in the hands of the few.

According to McGregor:

> Intellectual creativity cannot be "programmed" and directed the way we program and direct an assembly line or an accounting department. This kind of intellectual contribution to the enterprise cannot be obtained by giving orders, by traditional supervisory practices, or by close systems of control. Even conventional notions of productivity are meaningless with reference to the creative intellectual effort. Management has not yet considered in any depth what is involved in managing an organization heavily populated with people whose prime contribution consists of creative intellectual effort. (from Douglas McGregor's essay, "New Concepts of Management")

Here we have an idea from almost 60 years ago, which espouses the notion of creativity, the voice of the employee, collective intelligence, and engagement. However, we need to think about how this concept can be applied in today's environment where we have collaboration platforms, mobile devices, a younger generation of workers, and many of the other trends mentioned at the start of this book. This isn't just about getting rid of outdated management practices; it's about looking at how effective practices and ideas of the past can be updated to fit the world we work in today.

In addition to the great management thinkers, senior executives, and leaders that have been and are still around, we can't forget about the mid-level managers. Today there are many great managers who fight hard to support and empower their employees, encourage new ideas, and allow for workplace flexibility. There are some progressive and forward-thinking managers out there, but we need more people like that, much more.

One such manager is Tina[1] (real name redacted) who is now the executive director of business relationship management at a large cosmetics organization. In 2005 she was a manager on the 20-plus person service desk team that provided 24/7 support to more than 10,000 employees. To make things even more challenging, Tina's team members knew they were going to be outsourced in six months—talk about a tough spot to be in. Tina experimented and tried all sorts of ideas, such as giving employees the opportunities to nominate each other based on performance, hosting breakfast events or little parties, and dress-down days. Tina also spent one-on-one time with employees helping them fix up their resumes for future jobs (because they were all being outsourced). She had (and still has) a strong philosophy in standing up and backing her employees. This cosmetics company had a policy of doing merit raises every year, yet Tina petitioned for one employee to get a raise even though the employee was there for just six months. Human resources originally said no, so Tina had to fight and offered to give up her own bonus for one of her employees to get recognized. Eventually HR agreed to give the employee the raise and Tina was able to keep her bonus; the interesting thing is that this employee never even knew that Tina went to bat for her.

There are plenty of other things that she did but Tina didn't have to do any of these things, they weren't a part of her job description; instead she could have just "managed" people, but she didn't. She is a good example of the future manager, someone who believes in challenging assumptions, trying new ideas, and treating people like people. Tina regularly reads articles, books, and research on new management practices and employee engagement techniques and then she tries them. She recognized that things have changed and that she must change as well.

Another manager is Pamela Montana,[2] Americas inside sales center manager at Intel, where she has worked for nearly 13 years. Unlike the traditional model of a manager that sees Pamela as the boss and her employees as subordinates, Pamela sees her team of 16 employees as a family. This means that she isn't scared of being vulnerable with her team or sharing her mistakes. According to Pamela this is actually crucial to building trust. Interestingly, the majority of her team is located in Oregon while Pamela is in California, but she still has no trouble "managing" them. Instead of just focusing on yearly reviews Pamela focuses on weekly (or more often) check-ins to find out how her team is doing, what they might be struggling with, and how Pamela can help. She also has regular staff meetings every week; however, instead of starting each meeting by focusing on tasks, problems, or sales numbers Pamela starts off by focusing on recognition—what her employees were able to accomplish that week. Pamela recognizes that the world of work has changed and the role of managers is no longer about controlling and delegating. Her approaches and views are still considered novel today but they won't be for long.

Most companies are still run as though nothing has changed over the past few decades and they still implement and rely on management practices that, although may have been effective in the past, need to be rethought of and refreshed for the future. We need more Tinas and Pamelas working in our organizations.

In an article published in December of 2011 for the *Harvard Business Review* titled, "First, Let's Fire All the Managers,"[3] author and management consultant Gary Hamel wrote, "A small organization may have one manager and 10 employees; one with 100,000 employees and the same 1:10 span of control will have 11,111 managers. That's because an additional 1,111 managers will be needed to manage the managers." In the United Kingdom there are an estimated 5 million managers with around 30 million people employed, which means that more than 16 percent of the employed population in the United Kingdom is comprised of managers, which is considerably greater than the 10:1 ratio Gary Hamel wrote about (and which is assumed to be a standard in the United States). Clearly there are many millions of people around the world who are managers, but that doesn't have to be seen as a negative. It's not the fact that we have so many managers that's the problem—it's that the majority of managers are not adapting to the future of work, which is what the rest of this section is about.

In thinking of how to change and adapt we first have to understand a bit of background and context around the role of management and managers. Depending on how you view management it can either be traced as far as back as ancient Egypt, the industrial revolution in the eighteenth and nineteenth centuries, or to the more recent 20th century where people like Peter Drucker, Henri Fayol, Henry Gantt, and many others helped create and shape modern management. If we look at Henri Fayol, for example, his model for the functions of management was comprised of six functions (which he wrote in the late 1800s):

1. To forecast and plan
2. To organize
3. To command or direct
4. To coordinate
5. To develop output
6. To control

This sounds exactly like present-day management in many organizations.

It is during the twentieth century that most present-day management consultants, authors, and educators would say was the true creation of management. During this time, the first MBA program was introduced at the Tuck School of Business. Drucker actually discounted the notion of a command-and-control mentality decades ago and introduced the concept of respecting employees and treating them more like assets and less like liabilities. Now, many years later, we have seen some progress but not enough.

Managers used to be thought of as generals. They were the supreme commanders in the corporate world and everyone else had to do what they said. Managers had access to all the information, made decisions, and then delegated tasks to other employees. The original goal of a manager was to be a type of overseer. Managers needed to figure out how to keep their finely tuned machines running and generating as much money as possible. This meant getting employees to show up on time, work as many hours as possible, be as productive as possible while asking as few questions as possible, and basically just getting people to do their same repetitive jobs.

Managers didn't focus on or prioritize employee engagement, inspiration, giving employees a voice, creativity, or anything even remotely related to that. They didn't need to because none of the trends mentioned earlier, which are impacting the future of work today, existed. But as you saw in the previous section the future employee is different and the future manager must adapt. Years ago managers didn't have robots to do the work for them, so they employed human beings to do the jobs of robots instead, and this mentality has stuck with us today. We have to understand that as organizations started to grow so did the complexity surrounding those organizations. More people means more resources, more overhead, more interactions, more money, and more potential opportunities for success or failure. Someone needs to help make decisions and tell people what to do and steer the ship and that was the manager. However, eventually as organizations started to grow further those managers then needed managers of their own and then those managers needed their own managers. Before we knew it our organizations were constructed to reflect giant pyramids and a strict "pecking" order. How long can this type of an approach to work realistically continue? Another five years? Twenty years? Fifty years? One hundred years? Although some people imagine that it's hard for things to change, we should instead imagine how hard it would be for things *not* to change.

Now this doesn't mean that all managers today are controlling, treat employees like cogs, and don't believe in employee engagement. In fact far from it; however, it must be acknowledged that this is what modern management was built on top of. Some managers today are challenging these notions and are focusing on employee engagement, innovation, and creating desirable places to work.

Most managers think that the main reason why employees quit their jobs is because of salary. However, research consistently shows that the number one reason why employees leave companies is because of their bosses. Managers are actually a big factor in employee engagement and retention. In the 2013 Kelly Outsourcing and Consulting Group report "Employee Engagement and Retention"[4] participants were asked, "To what degree does your direct manager/supervisor impact your level of satisfaction or engagement with your employment?" They were asked to rate their responses on a scale of 1 to 5 where 5 had a significant impact and 1 had no impact. In the Americas 63 percent rated scored this at a 4 or a 5, in Europe, the Middle East, and Africa (EMEA) this was 60 percent, in the Asia Pacific APAC 68 percent, and the global average was 63 percent.

Thankfully, the traditional models and ideas of management are now being rethought, reexamined, and redesigned. In a world that moves as quickly as it does it's only safe to assume that management practices would evolve as well. Let's take a look at a few outdated management practices to get some context.

OUTDATED MANAGEMENT PRACTICES

The way we manage has virtually stayed the same over the past 150 to 200 years in many companies. In fact, most of the people who created and developed the management practices that we use today are no longer alive, yet for some reason we still subscribe to their outdated ideas and philosophies. These are ideas and approaches that have influenced everything from how we hire and onboard employees to how we run our companies. Here are just a few of the dated management practices today that are still considered the standard.

Hierarchies and Org Charts

According to Wikipedia, the first organizational chart was created by the Scottish-American engineer Daniel McCallum in 1854; for those of you keeping track that's around 160 years ago (however, hierarchies themselves go back thousands of years to ancient Egypt). These charts were widely adopted in the military to show the relationship between various personnel. They quickly made their way into organizations as well and have since become the standard for showing their structure. They were designed in a cascading way to show the senior level officers at the top and everyone else being depicted below them to show who reported to who. The assumption here is that information flows in a linear way "up or down the food chain."

Why It's Now Obsolete

Not only are new technologies making it easier for anyone within an organization to talk to anyone else but we are seeing a great push toward openness and transparency. Progressive organizations are trying to build cultures where employees are engaged, inspired, and creative. These organizations are also focusing on becoming agile and adaptable, which is completely contrary to the notion of a hierarchy.

Annual Reviews

If you're lucky, your organization offers annual or semi-annual reviews. In many organizations this is still an annual review. We've all been involved in the process where we sit down one-on-one with a manager and basically have to justify and explain why we deserve to get more money for the following year. We try to think of everything we have done and spend an hour or so trying to justify our cause. These reviews are often painful. Depending on who you listen to, this practice of annual/semi-annual reviews goes back from 70 to 200 years.

Why It's Now Obsolete

For the past 5 to 10 years we have been living in a connected and engaged world where providing feedback can now happen in real time with the click of a button. If an employee is working on something or requests feedback on something there is no reason why they need to wait six months or a year to have that discussion. New technologies and behaviors have made the notion of the annual or semi-annual review completely pointless. The analogy that's often used to help illustrate this point is sports. Imagine if you were the coach of a soccer or football team and after each game you waited six months to provide feedback and ideas on players' performance. Numerous studies also show that only around 5 percent of employees are satisfied with the reviews they get and the majority of HR managers actually dislike their own system! Achievers, a rewards and recognition consulting firm, did a study in 2012 of 645 HR managers: 98 percent of them believed that these types of reviews were not useful . . . 98 percent!

Adobe, which employs around 12,000 people, recently abandoned their annual review process in favor of more casual check-ins and conversations that happen in real time. According to Adobe, this is saving more than 80,000 employee hours a year.

Focusing on Inputs

The standard for measuring how productive or successful an employee is has always revolved around how many hours they spend doing something.

Not only that but managers wanted to physically see the employees coming into the office doing the work so that they would "know" that work was actually getting done. If you come in and put in your time then that's all that mattered.

Why This Is Now Obsolete

The future of work is about focusing on outputs. In other words, work when you want and where you want as long as you get your job done when you need to get it done and produce good-quality work. New technologies are making this possible and managers today are adjusting to this new way of work. There is simply no reason to focus on time spent working on something when the goal should be to focus on what is actually produced and how long it took to produce it.

Managers Have Access to Information and Make Decisions

Very much modeled after the military, the gold standard for how companies were run depended on the decisions that the managers made. These managers were the ones who had access to the information that was required to make decisions and once those decisions were made the tasks required to carry them out were delegated to the rest of the company. We saw this example earlier from Frederick Taylor and his approach to scientific management.

Why This Is Now Obsolete

We are seeing a massive shift toward opening up information and relying on collective intelligence and the wisdom of the crowds. It's becoming increasingly easier for employees to get access to people and information and these employees are able to come up with powerful ideas to help solve problems and identify new opportunities (think about Theory X and Theory Y).

There are many more outdated management practices, which I'm sure you can come up with. The thing to think about is why are they still being used today and why anything hasn't been done in most organizations to change them. We have become increasingly comfortable with the status quo and we need to step up and challenge that. It's time to really start questioning why certain things within our organizations are the way they are and how they can be changed for the better. It's time to start challenging convention.

The crucial issues with today's management boils down to a few things.

Too Few Controlling Too Much

As organizations grow and become more complex and as the rate of change in the world continues to accelerate, relying on just a few people to identify opportunities, avoid risks, and make decisions on behalf of the organization no longer becomes effective. Often, nonmanagerial employees are able to see the rocks on the horizon before the managers are.

No Room for Experimentation

Management is very formulaic, which is great if you are trying to put together Ikea furniture or run an organization in the 1900s. Traditional management approaches that our organizations have been built on top of don't allow for any wiggle room or experimentation to try new things. This means there is very little learning or adaptation as it relates to management. Management was taken as dogma with no room to challenge conventional wisdom.

Reliance on the Past

What worked in the past won't necessarily work in the future. Managers are running organizations today the same ways that managers did 100 years ago. The future manager needs to rely on future management practices not on ones from the past. If management practices of the past were focused on maintaining a finely oiled machine (keeping the status quo) then management practices of the future are about constantly building and adapting the machine (challenging convention).

Focusing on the Wrong Things

The emphasis on getting people to show up on time to do repetitive monotonous work day in and day out is no longer the focus of management, yet that is what management was created to do. The future of work sees an emphasis on the constant themes mentioned in this book such as innovation, adaptability, engagement, and creativity. Management was designed to oversee people who only worked with their hands; today, employees work with their minds as well.

CHAPTER **6**

Ten Principles of the Future Manager

Managers of the future are going to have to challenge the traditional ideas of management and push back against the many business practices that are outdated and no longer relevant. They will have to adapt to the future employee, which means new ways of working and thinking about work. In speaking with managers, many of them acknowledge that things are changing yet they aren't sure what those changes look like or what kind of a manager they should strive to become.

Figure 6.1 shows what these 10 principles of the future manager are. In order to adapt, the future manager:

- Must be a leader.
- Follow from the front.
- Understand technology.
- Lead by example.
- Embrace vulnerability.
- Believe in sharing and collective intelligence.
- Challenge convention and be a fire starter.
- Practice real-time recognition and feedback.
- Be conscious of personal boundaries.
- Adapt to the future employee.

10 PRINCIPLES OF
THE FUTURE MANAGER

10 ADAPTS TO THE FUTURE EMPLOYEE

1 IS A LEADER

2 FOLLOWS FROM THE FRONT

9 IS CONSCIOUS OF PERSONAL BOUNDARIES

3 UNDERSTANDS TECHNOLOGY

8 GIVES REAL-TIME RECOGNITION AND FEEDBACK

4 LEADS BY EXAMPLE

6 BELIEVES IN SHARING AND COLLECTIVE INTELLIGENCE

7 IS A FIRESTARTER

5 EMBRACES VULNERABILITY

© Chess Media Group

FIGURE 6.1   Ten Principles of the Future Manager

MUST BE A LEADER

If someone were to ask you, "Do we need more managers or more leaders?" what would you tell them? Most people would immediately say, "Of course, we need more leaders!" It's easy to see why most people would say this.

Typically managers are focused on enforcing control. They organize, oversee, supervise, delegate, and make sure things get done the right way and on time. However, often these managers may not be the best at inspiring or engaging employees, thinking outside of the box, challenging assumptions, or building trust; these are typically qualities that many associate with leaders. However, when it comes to the future of work these are all things they must get comfortable with because managers must be leaders.

If you had managers who were consistently improving the bottom line quarter after quarter but employees hated working for them would they be considered good managers? Similarly, if you worked for leaders who did an amazing job of engaging and inspiring employees but who failed to deliver any tangible results would they be considered to be good leaders? The answer to both of these is no. Remember that any employee has the potential to become a leader, but a manager who is responsible for other people must be a leader.

I believe this quote from business management author Henry Mintzberg rings true:

> Managers who don't lead are quite discouraging, but leaders who don't manage don't know what's going on. It's a phony separation that people are making between the two. (www.theglobeandmail.com/report-on-business/careers-leadership/mintzberg-real-leaders-don't-take-bonuses/article556910/?page=all and http://brainyquote.com/quotes/quotes/h/henrymintz528417.html)

In his 2014 book, *Leaders Eat Last: Why Some Teams Pull Together and Others Don't*, Simon Sinek points out that one of the most important qualities of leaders is that they must look after others and be willing to sacrifice themselves for others. In the workplace this means fighting for your employees and having the willingness to put yourself on the line to support them. As Sinek points out, leadership is a choice not a rank. This is a must-have quality and mind-set for the future manager. Managers must look after their employees, think of Tina's example earlier. Future managers cannot just be someone in a position of power who commands followers and enforces control. They must possess influence and they must earn followers.

There's an ongoing debate around whether we need more managers or more leaders but the reality is that what you call *them* makes no difference. Over the past few decades, thousands of pages have already been written on the difference between managers and leaders. There has been a painted divide between the two, which is now starting to disappear. Managers focus on "how," whereas leaders question "why." Managers control work and leaders guide people. Managers delegate and leaders listen. The manager focuses on profits and the leader focuses on prosperity. There are many such comparisons that have been drawn to separate the two as being different. However, painting managers as nonleaders does more harm than good. Instead the goal should be for managers to be leaders. It's unrealistic to think that organizations around the world are going to get rid of managers or somehow replace "managers" with "leaders." However, what is more realistic is helping organizations understand the potential of what their managers can and should become.

The dictionary definitions of both *manager* and *leader* are almost identical, yet the perception that most of us have is that managers are like police officers and leaders are visionaries who help shape the world. What's required isn't a new title or a description but a different way of thinking; it's this new way of thinking that most people associate with being a leader. The bottom line is that we need fewer people who exert control and manage work and more people who inspire, engage, challenge, and lead people; this is exactly who the future manager will be.

At Whirlpool,[1] for example, managers are referred to as "people leaders." The expectation is that everyone should lead, and the Whirlpool Leadership Model defines specific behaviors based on different levels of leadership scope: those who are leaders based on their individual contributions (leading self), those who lead other people in a team (leading others), those who lead a plant or department (leading function), and those who lead at the executive level (leading enterprise). This is an approach that all organizations can emulate by defining the types of leaders that are required and desired to create an organization ready for the future of work.

The future manager must be a leader.

FOLLOWING FROM THE FRONT

The notion of managers doing any type of following is a foreign concept to many people. Traditionally it was the manager who was out front with the employees following behind or perhaps more accurately, the managers were at the top of the pyramid while the employees were at the bottom.

Following from the front flips this idea on its head. In other words, when it comes to the future of work, the goal of managers is to remove roadblocks from the paths of employees in order to help them succeed while empowering them to work in a way that makes them engaged and effective. Today, many managers still have the "How can I get the most out of my employees" mind-set instead of the "What can I do to help employees be most effective and engaged?" mind-set. The managers are holding up the pyramid, not standing on top of it.

Thinking back to what we now know about the future employee it's not hard to see why a command-and-control or fear-based approach to management is now obsolete.

Managers need to realize that their role is to serve the employees and not the other way around (the way it used to be). Managers exist not to police and control employees but to support them, coach them, and enable them. This is what enables employees to then become leaders themselves.

Let's take two scenarios to see how they compare. In both scenarios we can assume that you work for a mid-size or even a large-size company.

In scenario A you are a project manager and are currently working on a new initiative that requires you to assemble a team, build a case to get resource approval, and create a strategy. The traditional approach to something like this would be that a manager works with an employee to craft deliverables, timelines, and hopefully set reasonable expectations. From there it's up to the employee to deliver. In other words, the manager is assigned the task and the employee executes the task. Hopefully in a few weeks the employee would deliver.

In scenario B everything is the same except now the manager takes the approach of following from the front. This can be seen in several ways. First, the manager already knows about a few potential people who might be a good fit for the team; second, the manager gives his peers a heads-up about the new project and asks them to help support the employee; third, the manager empowers the employee to make any project decisions without having to always get approval or feedback from the manager. Fourth, the manager plays a proactive role in following the progress, relevant conversations, and developments of the project through technology such as a collaboration platform.

The actions that the manager takes can vary greatly. The most important thing for the future manager is to constantly be in that mindset of "How can I support and empower employees?" instead of "What tasks should I be assigning to employees?"

Following from the front implies that the manager is running ahead of the ship clearing a path for the employee to move through. To use an analogy, it's akin to having someone build a tunnel through a mountain for you to move through instead of your having to traverse through the mountain yourself. There is still plenty of work that the employee needs to do, though. In this example the manager could allow employees to make budgetary decisions, connect them with people who might be a good fit for the team, or provide an example of a strategy. The manager here plays a much more supporting role to empower the employees and help them succeed. This can include everything mentioned earlier to providing a heads-up to other managers about this new project, listening and following along via a company collaboration platform, and doing other things behind the scenes to help make the life of the employee easier.

The time has come to move beyond fear-based management tactics and instead focus on engaging, inspiring, and empowering those who work with us. Often we hear that the best way to get promoted or recognized is to make your manager look good. But what about the nonmanagerial employees? Instead of taking this approach it's up to the future manager to make their employees look good!

Employees are the most valuable asset that an organization possesses, and managers who follow from the front recognize and act on that.

UNDERSTANDING TECHNOLOGY AND HOW EMPLOYEES WORK

The future manager must be on top of what is happening in the world of technology. Having an understanding of technology doesn't mean knowing how to set up a server, develop a product, or code a website. Managers don't need to become IT professionals. But, with the pace of technological change today it is important for managers to be able to stay on top of the trends, the technology landscape, and how it may impact the world of work.

This is a new concept because traditionally anything related to technology was always left up to the IT department, but thanks to cloud-based technologies, all of that has changed. Anyone can be up and running with powerful business software in just a few minutes, whether it be a manager or a first day on the job employee. This means that future managers need to understand how new technologies can be leveraged to help empower employees. Managers also need to understand how employees work to help identify if and where technology can be used.

Different business problems require different technologies. In my previous book, *The Collaborative Organization*, I laid out a framework for developing use cases and evaluating various technology vendors.

The technology landscape can be quite vast, but here are a few areas to help get started.

Collaboration Platforms

There are hundreds of collaboration platforms and new ones are springing up all the time. These platforms are valuable for connecting and engaging people and information anywhere, anytime, and on any device. It's also one of the key components of maintaining a flexible work environment. Being able to follow the key trends and developments here is crucial for the future of work.

Project and Task-Management Platforms

Sometimes these fall under collaboration platforms but there are a growing number of stand-alone applications that specifically focus on what is now being called *social* task or project management. These tools allow managers and employees to make sure that teams are aligned, work is getting done, and feedback and insight are being shared with the relevant people.

Social Learning Systems

Learning used to be done via an employee handbook and a projector in a dimly lit room. Today new learning systems are allowing employees to take control of how they learn. Employees now have the ability to not only learn from each other but can also teach other. New learning technologies make it easy for employees to act as both teachers and students. This is important to follow for onboarding of new employees and talent development.

Video

Most people would probably not expect to find video here but it's actually becoming a huge factor in how employees work, especially when considering flexible work environments and telepresence. Managers should be aware of how video can be used to impact how employees work, learn, educate each other, communicate, and collaborate. In a recent survey of 1,300 executives age 34 and younger called "The 2013 Cisco Global Young Executives' Video Attitudes Survey,"[2] 87 percent said that they believe video has a significant positive impact on the organization. Three out of five of the respondents said that they will rely on business class video over the next 5 to 10 years. Another 87 percent said that they would choose to work for a video-enabled organization over a company that has not invested in business-class video communications.

There are clearly plenty of other areas that can be followed as well (such as CRM or gamification), but as far as the future of work goes I believe these to be some of the key areas. When thinking about technology it's also important to remember not to go overboard. Deploying a lot of new technologies frequently can cause problems, which is why it's so important for managers to understand how employees actually work. The last thing you want to happen is for employees to get overwhelmed and burned out on technology.

Staying up-to-date on technology trends is also a fairly straightforward and easy task. It can include everything from attending industry conferences and events, to reading books and blogs, to having ongoing conversations with peers. The point is to stay plugged in.

Managers who understand what is happening with technology and the world of work will always have an advantage over those who don't. This is key for being able to adapt and evolve. In the last section of this book technology is explored further.

LEAD BY EXAMPLE

Supporting a project or initiative usually meant that executives would publicly state or show their support. This could be done where an executive sends around a short video of himself saying that he supports something, it could be done in a town-hall style meeting, or perhaps even in an internal newsletter. Often, supporting something just meant providing budgetary approval and then doing some action to show support.

When it comes to the future of work, sharing, collaborating, and open communication, support must go deeper. Let's take the example of a company rolling out a new collaboration technology for a company to use.

A company can either roll out the technology, make an announcement about it, have the senior leaders make a video or write an article about its value, and then go on their merry way. Or, a company can actually have its executive teams use and participate in the platforms themselves. This means engaging with employees, sharing content, listening to what is going on within the organization, and being present. This isn't something that takes much time, either. With a simple Internet connection a manager or executive can easily be in touch with employees via a mobile device while sitting in a cab or even standing in line at a coffee shop. It just takes effort and commitment.

Jack Welch did an excellent job of this when he was running General Electric by creating and introducing the concept of the boundaryless organization. He wanted to be able to empower all employees, not just managers, throughout the organization to come up with ideas and solve problems. He didn't want boundaries of any kind to exist within his organization whether they were departmental or hierarchical. The fascinating thing about this is that it was more than just talk. Jack led by example and actually made the time to sit with his employees and learn about new ideas and solutions that employees might have had. Today, collaborative technologies make this process of breaking down boundaries and empowering employees much easier and more effective. I should also point out that Jack also implemented and was the creator of the stack-ranking system mentioned earlier, which many consider to be outdated now.

Support isn't just about providing funding for something or making an appearance. Support is about actually changing and showing everyone that you are changing. In the world of collaboration this can easily be seen by managers using the same collaborative platforms that they encourage their employees to use. If managers don't use them then why should employees?

EMBRACE VULNERABILITY

Most people assume that vulnerability is weakness because that's how the word is typically used. Sports teams want to exploit vulnerabilities of their opponents, we want to find and remove software vulnerabilities in our computer systems, we never want to find out about structural vulnerabilities, and people who are vulnerable are easy to take advantage of. In fact, if there is one thing that managers think they shouldn't be, it's vulnerable. Men especially go through their whole lives learning how to be the opposite of vulnerable. Growing up in a Russian household, I can tell you that I experienced this firsthand. This typically meant not crying, being strong and fiercely competitive.

However, Brene Brown, author of *Daring Greatly: How the Courage to Be Vulnerable Transforms the Way We Live, Love, Parent, and Lead*, says that vulnerability is about having the courage to show up and be seen. According to Brown, "Vulnerability is the absolute heartbeat of innovation and creativity. There can be zero innovation without vulnerability."

Most of us assume the vulnerability is a weakness but the reality is that being vulnerable is about being human—it's what allows us to connect with other people. This is especially relevant in a work setting.

My favorite example of this comes from Peter Aceto,[3] CEO of Tangerine (formerly ING Direct Canada), an online bank that has around 1,000 employees in Canada. When Peter first started working at Tangerine more than 10 years ago, he portrayed the typical executive— not very emotional, seemingly always in control, and a bit robotic. One day Peter's boss (who was more like a coach or mentor), pulled him aside and told him that this wasn't who he really was. Peter's mentor knew about his family, his tumultuous relationship with his father, the fact that he liked hockey, and all sorts of other things about Peter. Yet for some reason Peter was trying to hide who he really was at work. His mentor said he liked the real Peter and encouraged him to show up at Tangerine. Peter is genuinely open and transparent and he felt as though he was given permission to be himself, and that's exactly what he did. In speaking with Peter, he shared how liberating it was to be able to be the same person at work and at home without having to expend energy to pretend to be someone else.

For Peter this was more than just about being himself, it was also about building high-performance teams and running a thriving company. He noticed around 20 to 30 percent more productivity and volunteerism (based on observation) in addition to improved employee engagement. As more people took Peter's lead and also embraced vulnerability, employees actually started enjoying coming to work more and when they were at work they gave everything they had. Peter also noticed that innovation was rapidly increasing because more engaged employees meant more ideas that they were willing to contribute.

Engagement levels at Tangerine are almost at 90 percent, which is very high. At Tangerine, engagement is defined as: "The emotional connection, the passion and pride, that an employee feels toward both their work and their employer." The company measures this by asking employees to rank their responses to statements on a six-point scale ranging from strongly disagree to strongly agree. The six statements are:

1. Overall, I am proud to work for Tangerine.
2. I am committed to Tangerine.
3. I would gladly refer a friend or family member to Tangerine for employment.
4. My work gives me a sense of personal accomplishment.
5. I am willing to work beyond what is required to help Tangerine succeed.
6. I would prefer to stay with Tangerine if I was offered a similar job elsewhere.

When I asked Natasha Mascarenhas, the head of HR at Tangerine, why she and her team care about engagement her response was simple, "We are only as good as our people."

To build a competitive and thriving organization you have to have the best people. Top talent requires an environment where people trust one another, where they share, where employees are engaged, and where employees can be open and vulnerable.

As Peter often mentions, business is built on relationships whether it be with employees or customers. You can't have meaningful real relationships with either employees or customers if you are scared to be vulnerable or show emotion. People want to work with people, not with robots. The moral of the story is that when you embrace vulnerability good things happen to you and your organization.

BELIEF IN SHARING AND COLLECTIVE INTELLIGENCE

Traditionally, managers sat at the top of the organizational hierarchy and had access to all of the information required to make decisions. Managers would then make the decisions and then dole out the orders that the employees had to execute. This is a bit ironic because managers and executives are the people farthest from the so-called ground-floor of the organization. These aren't the people who build the products, service the customers, or write the code. It's a bit silly when you think about it, because ultimately managers make predictions for when things need to get done, they assign timelines, tasks, milestones, and (my favorite) deliverables based on what they believe or think they know.

Today this mentality is not only ineffective, it's actually harmful to the organization. The future manager believes in collective intelligence— that is, tapping into the wisdom, experience, ideas, and knowledge of their team(s) or the company as a whole.

Consider an experiment that DARPA (a research division of the U.S. Department of Defense) ran in 2009. The basic gist of the experiment was that 10 giant red weather balloons were released in random locations in the United States. Teams from various universities entered the competition; the first team to correctly find all 10 balloons won $40,000. How long do you think it would take to do something like this? Consider how this would have even been possible at all 10 years ago. MIT won the contest in just around nine hours. DARPA was prepared to keep the challenge open for around a week and were quite surprised by the result. So how did MIT find these balloons? In short, through collective intelligence. They relied on social media along with an incentive program they created. See Figure 6.2.

We can see from Figure 6.2 how the size of an engaged network dramatically increases the value that the network can provide and the complexity of the problems that can be solved. Now imagine something like this within your organization. Think of the problems your organization can solve, the opportunities it can collectively identify, and the products that people can come up with.

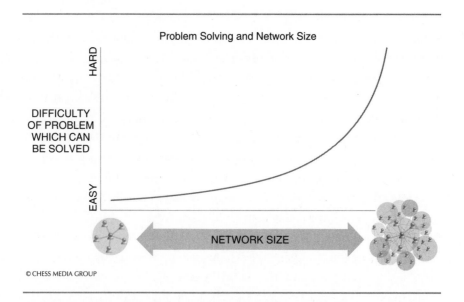

FIGURE 6.2   **Problem Solving and Network Size**

We actually use collective intelligence all the time in our personal lives. Think of a question you may have put out on Twitter, or a problem you were looking to solve by polling your Facebook friends.

The reason why collective intelligence is powerful is because of our ability to create weak ties, as seen in Figure 6.3.

Weak ties allow us to get access to people and information that we would otherwise not have access to. Chances are the people in our direct network (strong ties) have access to the same people and information that we do, so they can't always be as helpful. A weak tie acts as a bridge, which means new ideas, new information, new solutions, and new knowledge and expertise. Managers traditionally relied on decision making from their direct network (their strong ties), whereas the weak ties become extremely important in the future of work.

Collective intelligence can be used for anything ranging from ideas to cutting costs, the identification of new opportunities or marketing,

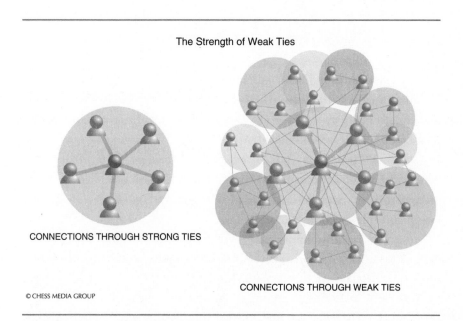

The Strength of Weak Ties

CONNECTIONS THROUGH STRONG TIES

CONNECTIONS THROUGH WEAK TIES

© CHESS MEDIA GROUP

FIGURE 6.3   The Strength of Weak Ties

or simple things such as getting help on a problem or asking a question. The point is to rely on the intelligence of many instead of the intelligence of a few.

Game maker Electronic Arts (EA) uses the wisdom of employees to help accurately predict which games will be more successful so it knows where to allocate dollars. Henkel, the global manufacturing company of chemical products, uses collective intelligence to improve sales forecasts (which it did by 22 percent). Small and large organizations around the world are realizing the value of tapping into the wisdom of their employees to help solve problems and make decisions.

Today, managers cannot believe in hoarding information but in sharing information and collective intelligence. Managers need to make sure that the employees can connect to each other and to the information they need to get their jobs done, anytime, anywhere, and on any device. Managers now rely on employees to help make decisions instead of isolating them from this process.

BE A FIRE STARTER

Management used to be very formulaic. There was a template for how managers needed to act, how they needed to supervise, how they needed to discipline employees, and how they needed to get things done. Sadly, this is a template that has remained very much unchanged over the years. In fact, many people refer to these types of managers as *cookie-cutter managers*. That is, they approach everything the same way with the same process, after all, that's what used to make a good manager and what still makes a good cookie.

Managers of the future must challenge conventional ideas about management and work and not just take things at face value—they must be curious. The future manager must ditch the template and the management formula. We see this approach in chess quite frequently. Players often prepare opening moves; that is, the first few moves that each player makes at the start of a game. But once the game approaches the middle game (after the prepared initial moves are made) the players are on their own. They are forced to find unique combinations, adapt to new scenarios, and try to figure out the best next move. Managers need to look at work the same way. There might be some initial guidelines or approaches that can be used, but at the end of the day it's up to the managers to come up with new ideas, approaches, and theories; and there's nothing wrong with testing them to see what happens. Experimentation is a manager's best friend.

Although this notion of being a fire starter is also true for employees, it's especially relevant for managers who may most likely be the ones leading teams and companies. It's their behavior that many employees will likely emulate and so if the managers exhibit and encourage this kind of behavior then employees will likely adopt it as well.

- Is a hierarchy really the best structure for my team or company?
- Do my employees really benefit from getting a review every six months?
- Why can't employees be a part of the decision-making process just like managers?
- Why do employees need to commute to work in an office?
- How can I better serve my employees instead of having them serve me?

These are some of the questions that managers of the future will be asking themselves. Part of being a fire starter is understanding how work is currently done and challenging the assumptions and ideas associated with that to come up with some different, more effective, and hopefully better. None of this can be accomplished without testing and trying things out. It's not hard to do this either. In fact, that's how many of the organizations featured in this book started. At Cisco flexible work didn't start with a corporate-wide initiative to all 75,000-plus employees. Instead a few employees just started working from home to avoid commuting, other employees worked from home because Cisco opened remote offices, and still others were always on the road. Eventually this became a standard practice at Cisco.

Try ditching the formal review process, let employees work from home, or invite employees into managerial meetings to get their feedback. These are simple, inexpensive, and low-risk things that any manager can do. The future manager will spend a lot more time asking "why" and "how can this done better."

REAL-TIME RECOGNITION, FEEDBACK, AND ENGAGEMENT

As mentioned earlier, the notion of the semi-annual or annual employee review dates back many decades and is still accepted and used as the standard for evaluating employees today. This process is infrequent and can often take several hours to complete. It relies on a standard process that all managers need to follow and doesn't really focus on the employee as a person. It's like an assembly line where employees come in, plead their case, get their review, walk out, and the next one walks in. Great for robots, not so good for people. This process is also usually one directional which very much fits with the hierarchical model where orders flow from the top to the bottom.

Today collaboration platforms allow managers and employees to provide real-time recognition, feedback, and engagement. All of these things are now bi-directional.

Recognition

If you wanted to recognize an employee at your job for doing something now, would you do it? Chances are you would somehow contact the employee directly and say, "Good job." Maybe this can happen the same day, the same week, or whenever it's convenient. If the employee is lucky, maybe he or she will get featured in a company newsletter or get a plaque on a wall somewhere.

Now consider Medium,[4] a blog-publishing platform started by Evan Williams, one of the founders of Twitter. The company developed a technology called High Five where anyone within the company can "high-five" anyone else for a job well done. These "high-fives" are then broadcast for the whole company to see. I visited the offices in San Francisco and saw employees giving each other real-time recognition on everything from technical coding, to marketing, to operations-related tasks. All of these things happen in real time. Not only does the employee get the recognition but the other employees also see that their peer was recognized. This method is scalable, open to anyone, easy to use, and effective.

Shopify, an e-commerce site, does something similar with an internal platform it created called Unicorn, which allows employees to crowd-source their bonuses. Employees can assign Unicorns to coworkers (analogous to the high-fives that Medium uses) and at the end of each month bonuses are proportioned to the number of Unicorns that an employee has received. Just like with Medium, this process is open, transparent, scalable, and easy to join.

According to a report published by Achievers in June of 2012 called "The State of Employee Recognition in 2012,"[5] less than 20 percent of employees are recognized monthly or more often. The same report cites that the U.S. Department of Labor found that 64 percent of working Americans leave their jobs because they do not feel appreciated. More interestingly, 87 percent of organizations have recognition programs that specifically focus on tenure—in other words, the longer you stay with the company the more recognition and appreciation you get. The focus for most of these programs has nothing to do with work produced, results generated, helping coworkers, or anything else related to these things. The future employee specifically craves and wants recognition and feedback so this is also a method of being able to attract and retain top talent within organizations. Unfortunately, most organizations today simply don't have anything in place that allows for effective peer or even manager recognition in real time and across boundaries. Today technology solutions exist to help solve this very problem.

The fact that this type of recognition opens up communication lines inside the company is a powerful thing. Think of how an entry level employee might feel if they share something only to find that the CEO of the company just "liked the update." The employee will be excited, engaged, and valued. A few years ago this type of thing would be unheard of.

Recognition doesn't need to wait, it happens in real time.

Feedback

Perhaps you have an employee who is working on a client presentation who is also looking for some feedback; again, he shares the presentation and moments later starts getting real-time feedback on missing data, perhaps some additional information that he should include, and maybe someone even responds with some additional ideas to add.

Imagine an employee who just comes back from a client meeting who shares an update with his team that says, "just closed a deal with company XYZ, it's not as big as I was hoping for but it's a step in the right direction." A manager can quickly pick up on this and respond with something like, "Great job, keep up the good work." This simple comment provides real-time feedback to the employee helping him get recognized and showing him that he is appreciated. Managers or employees can do this from their desktops, laptops, or even mobile devices.

Not all feedback needs to be positive, real-time feedback can come in many forms, including constructive criticism. There's nothing wrong with saying something like, "The report needs a bit more work, can you please revise sections A & B" or "We didn't handle that client as well as we should have, here are some things for us to work on for next time."

This type of real-time feedback, recognition, or engagement can be collected and provided on a variety of topics, including how employees are feeling at work, what they are working on, something they are sharing, or a problem they might have. Some vendors even have little faces that employees can click on to share how they are feeling throughout the day, thus giving direct feedback of the company or the team mood.

The manager of the future won't wait six months or a year to recognize employees or provide feedback, the manager of the future will do it in real time.

CONSCIOUS OF PERSONAL BOUNDARIES

The future manager must be conscious of boundaries. When it comes to the future of work we are always connected and so this can also pose several challenges. There are several boundaries that managers must know how to balance and be aware of.

Time

As we continue to connect our organizations it becomes increasingly harder to "switch-off." This idea of always being connected is taken by many to assume it means "always available." Just because we are connected doesn't mean that we are available and that is a boundary that managers need to help encourage. Our professional and personal lives are starting to blur greatly, and for some today there is already no distinction. Many employees bring their personal lives to work and their work lives home to their personal lives. In fact in an April 6, 2012 article by the *Huffington* Post called, "Sheryl Sandberg: 'There's No Such Thing As Work-Life Balance,'"[6] Sandberg was quoted as saying: "So there's no such thing as work-life balance. There's work, and there's life, and there's no balance."

All employees and managers within an organization need to be empowered to create their own balance, but this can largely be influenced from managers. Often, employees get invited to 6 A.M. meetings with international team members, get asked to join phone calls at 10 P.M., get requests to finish up projects on weekends, and sometimes even get tasked with getting things done while they are on vacation with family.

The temptation to do this is there, but it's a temptation that needs to be fought against. Just because we are always connected doesn't mean we are always available. This is the quickest way to get burned out and start to resent your job and the people you work with. Difficulty in being able to disconnect can result in personal and professional difficulties such as:

- Not enough time to spend with friends and family.
- Getting burned out at work.
- Becoming disengaged and a workplace zombie.
- Stress and personal health issues.

An article published by *Engadget* on April 9, 2014 called, "No Work Emails After 6 P.M. Please, We're French,"[7] cites that earlier in 2014 a legally binding document was signed by several technology employers and unions in France which prohibits many companies from actually electronically contacting their employees after the work day is over. A few months before that in late 2013, the German Labor Ministry banned managers from calling or emailing employees out of business hours, except in emergencies. In both of these situations one of the primary reasons for these bans was to avoid burnout. One of the biggest difficulties that stems from this is the setting of expectations. If managers consistently assume that employees are available just because they are connected and if employees consistently accept those meeting invites and weekend projects, then this eventually sets the expectation that this is okay and it becomes an ongoing reality. This means more early morning calls and late night projects; it starts to snowball. Managers and employees need to work together to identify and set realistic expectations early on. If it gets to the point where things become very one-sided then perhaps the employee is not a good fit for the current role or the employee is being given an unreasonable amount of work with unrealistic expectations for completion.

A few months ago while letting my dog Athena play in a park I met a guy who used to work in the corporate world (in finance I believe). We talked for a bit and I asked him what he was up to now. He said he was recovering. Naturally I was curious and probed further (perhaps inappropriately). The guy told me that the company he worked for was constantly putting pressure on him to work above and beyond what he was supposed to. One day he was driving his car in the Bay Area on the freeway and blacked out. His car flipped over multiple times and crashed into the center divider. Paramedics came and found him dead, he had to be revived. He told me that doctors said stress was the primary cause for his blackout and heart attack.

Miki Chan, the lady who provides dog-grooming services for my dog used to work in the corporate sector as well. She was high up the "food chain" and although she liked her job, she recognized the toll that work was taking on her life. So she quit and started a dog-grooming service called Spago Dog, where she does what she loves and works around 40 hours a week.

This type of burnout and being overworked has happened even before we lived in a connected world, which is why it's so crucial for managers and employees to be mindful of it now because the ability for it happen in the future will increase dramatically.

Space

The second type of boundary that managers need to be aware of is that of space. Working in a connected and collaborative world sometimes makes it hard to distinguish and separate between "friend" and "coworker." Information travels faster and can reach a much larger group of people within the company (and externally). It's not so much that we need to be conscious of not mingling the two to together; we just need to aware that the two relationships are different.

Many employees, for example, may find it uncomfortable to get Facebook friend requests from their managers or even coworkers. I've spoken with many employees at several companies who find it a bit unsettling that their managers send them friend requests on social channels even though they don't want to accept them. It might sound silly, but it's a bit of a tricky situation for many employees. Do they accept the request from their manager and open up their personal lives or do they ignore the request and hope the manager doesn't notice? In their 2013 report called, "Business Etiquette: The New Rules in a Digital Age,"[8] which surveyed almost 1,400 senior managers at companies in the United States and Canada, professional staffing firm Robert Half found that 47 percent are "not comfortable" at all about being friended by their boss. Furthermore, 33 percent echoed the same response when being asked about being friended by coworkers, 40 percent about people they manage, and 51 percent about clients. Still, 39 percent of the senior managers said they are somewhat comfortable about being friended by their coworkers.

This is obviously a personal choice but the key here is to just be aware that many people might prefer to connect with colleagues or managers on more professional channels such as LinkedIn or not at all. Privacy settings do exist for things like this, but how many of us actually take the time to group our contacts into categories or groups, or to assign visibility to specific "friends"?

In person it's much easier to keep this separation, a manager or coworker won't just randomly show up at your house and knock on your door or call you up out of the blue to share a personal story (okay, maybe sometimes). But when it comes to social media this separation is much harder to acknowledge and respect. Again, there is no right or wrong approach, the goal is for managers (and employees) to just be aware that in a connected world we need to be aware of these things.

ADAPT TO THE FUTURE EMPLOYEE

Because the employee of the future is changing, the manager of the future must change and adapt as well. The future employee brings a new idea of what it means to work and if this new way of working is met with an old way of managing then it will result in a lot of tension and frustration. It's like trying to put together two puzzle pieces that don't fit. To adapt to the future employee, the future manager must:

- Follow from the front
- Understand technology
- Lead by example
- Embrace vulnerability
- Believe in sharing and collective intelligence
- Challenge convention and be a fire starter
- Practice real-time recognition and feedback
- Be conscious of personal boundaries

In a dynamic and rapidly changing world, organizations simply cannot afford to have a gap between how employees expect and need to work and how managers lead. This means that managers must need to understand the underlying trends outlined in this book as well as the new realities of the future of work.

EVOLUTION OF THE MANAGER

To better understand all the ways in which managers are changing the way they operate, take a look at Figure 6.4.

What Now?

Figure 6.4 is a model for the future manager, but I encourage you to adapt it, add to it, and modify it as you see fit. What I have included are

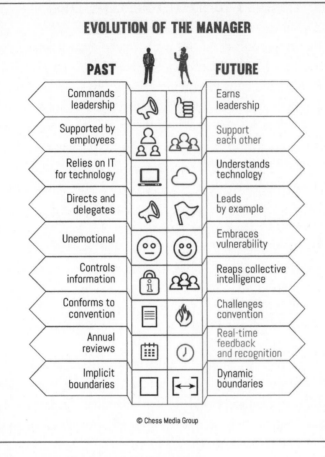

FIGURE 6.4 Evolution of the Manager

some of the most crucial characteristics that I have found, but they are by no means the only ones. How the future manager adapts and changes is going to be different for every organization and every manager but the point is that change needs to happen.

It's not hard to see why the current ideas and approaches to management need to change. They are completely out of sync with the way the future employee is going to work. Thankfully many organizations around the world are recognizing this and are taking steps to help close the gap. It's not a question of *if* approaches to management are going to change, it's a question of *when*, and the answer is "now."

Now that we have a picture for the future manager, where do we go from here and how do these future managers make their way into our organizations? We will see a few things happen.

Natural Shift

At the beginning of the book a telling statistic was cited and I'll repeat it here: "63.3 percent of U.S. executives will be eligible to retire in the next five years and 33 percent are currently eligible to retire." Again as mentioned earlier, in the past five years: 87 percent of millennial workers took on management roles, versus 38 percent of Gen X and just 19 percent of boomers. This means that in the next few years we will end up seeing a natural shift of new managers entering the workplace who will bring about new behaviors and new approaches to leading and running organizations. It will take a few years for this to happen but it will be a natural progression.

Some Will Adapt, Others Won't

Some managers "get it," which means that they fully understand that they need to change and adapt to the future employee and to the future of work. Still, many managers don't believe that change is necessary. They believe that command and control, "butts in seats," and strict hierarchy is still the way that work must get done. I remember speaking with a global organization with hundreds of thousands of employees where everyone was asked to wear a suit and tie to work every day, even though most of the jobs weren't customer facing. Although this might sound like a trivial thing it does impact corporate culture. When I asked why this was the case I was told, "That's what the CEO wants and he said it has to be that way until the day he dies." These are the types of managers and executives who don't have much of a place in the future organization.

They will have to adapt or they will disappear because nobody will want to work for them or the organizations that they manage.

HIRING AND PROMOTING THE RIGHT PEOPLE

However you choose to structure your organization, it's crucial that the people who become managers or leaders must be the right people for the job. In investment firms, for example, those who brought in the most money were typically promoted to the role of VP or SVP, which inherently meant that they managed a team of employees. This is a horrible approach for management. Just because someone brings in the most amount of money doesn't mean they make a good manager. Organizations need to be extremely conscious of who they decide to put in management or leadership roles and they must ask themselves, "Are these the qualities that we want to instill within our company?" The qualities of the future manager described earlier is a great place to start.

Education and Training

Even managers need mentors and coaches to help them be better. However, these coaches don't have to be hired help, they can be other employees within the organization. In fact, several companies such as TELUS and IBM have put in place reverse mentoring programs where employees who "get it" can mentor managers or executives who are still trying to figure out how new behaviors and technologies are impacting the workplace. Training sessions, lunch and learns, presentations with guest speakers, and workshops are all being used to better help prepare and educate existing and potential managers. Resources such as this book are designed for this exact educational reason.

CHAPTER 7

The Managerless Company

Sun Hydraulics is a 900-person publicly traded company founded in 1970 that designs and makes screw-in hydraulic cartridge valves and manifolds used in fluid power systems. Over the past decade the share price of Sun Hydraulics has increased by around 1,800 percent going from $2.20 to just over $41 dollars a share. Valve, mentioned earlier, is a 400-person gaming company valued at around $4 billion and has a 98 percent employee retention rate. Their profitability per employee is higher than that of Google, Amazon, or Microsoft. Medium is a platform for content discovery and storytelling that was started by one of the co-founders of Twitter, Evan Williams, and the company has around 40 people based in San Francisco. Treehouse has around 100 people; the company helps people learn web design and development and helps people find technical jobs; and since its creation more than three years ago has lost only three people. W. L. Gore, creator of the Gore-Tex fabric, has more than 10,000 employees and is consistently ranked in *Fortune*'s 100 Best Companies to Work For annual list. Supercell, the Finnish gaming company with more than 100 employees is valued at around $3 billion and makes $2.5 million a day and recently raised $1.5 billion (with a "B") in funding (for a 51 percent stake in the company to Soft-Bank and GungHo). Morning Star is the world's largest tomato processor with around 2,500 employees headquartered in Woodland, California. GitHub is a collaboration platform for software developers, which is currently used by more than 3 million people. The company employs around 250 people and recently raised $100 million in venture capital from Andreessen-Horowitz. Automattic, the company that created the popular blogging platform WordPress has around 200 employees who mainly work remotely in around 30 countries and 150 cities around the world. The company has more than a $1 billion valuation. Zappos, which was acquired by Amazon for more than $1 billion a few years ago, currently has more than 1,500 employees and is known around the world for their amazing workplace culture

All of these companies have something in common. There are no managers. Actually, that's not entirely true. Sun Hydraulics does have an honorary "plant manager," however, this isn't the type of role you think it is. At the Sun machine shop they have a massive building with hundreds of living plants hanging from the ceiling, the plant manager is the person responsible for taking care of the plants. But aside from that, no managers! The idea of the managerless company is often associated with a style of running an organization known as holacracy whose primary focus rests on the idea of distributed decision making and self-organization.

So how do these organizations get anything done if there are no managers? All of the companies mentioned earlier have slightly different approaches and tweaks to the way they operate, so although they share the "no manager" approach there are some unique qualities of each.

HOW DO EMPLOYEES GET HIRED OR FIRED?

When it comes to hiring (and firing), Valve has a communal approach. Let's say you realize that you need a software developer, you reach out to some of your colleagues to see if they feel the same way, put together a search committee that anyone can be a part of, and then start the virtual and then in-person interview process. When the search committee members feel that the right person has been found, they agree and bring them in; no manager approval required. The same approach is taken when it comes to letting someone go, if there is a sense that someone doesn't fit at the company then there is a group discussion among peers to see if anything can be done to solve the problem, if not then the person is asked to leave. At Valve, this usually happens not because of performance issues but because the person just doesn't fit with the Valve corporate culture. Automattic has a similar process but it also hires employees on a trial that lasts around three to eight weeks to see how the prospective employee can work within Automattic, if all goes well the position becomes permanent. The communal hiring process has been quite consistent at Sun Hydraulics, Gore, and the rest of the organizations mentioned earlier. It's usually a team or group effort and not a decision that is just left up to an HR professional or executive. Often, if someone wants to sit in or participate in the hiring process, they can. Usually the team members who will be working with the new candidate end up interviewing them along with any of the "executives."

HOW DO EMPLOYEES FIGURE OUT WHAT PROJECTS TO WORK ON?

The approach for deciding what to work on is relatively similar across all the companies mentioned earlier, and it's quite simple. Employees decide! Employees can either ask each other what projects are going on or often there are internal project lists and voting systems, which the company uses, all web-based. So as a new employee I can easily see what projects are going on in the company and decide which one(s) I want to be a part of. Similarly, if I have an idea for a project I want to start, it's my responsibility to put the project up on the platform, tell people about it, and recruit a team to get started. If I can't get the interest and the people to work on the project, then it doesn't happen. This approach sounds like it makes sense for a technology or an online company like Treehouse or GitHub, but what about for a manufacturing company like W. L. Gore, Sun Hydraulics, or Morning Star? At Gore, facilities are limited to around 200 people, after that, a new one is created. Each facility also has a mix of engineers, salespeople, machinists, and many other roles. Instead of anybody telling you what to do, peers negotiate assignments and responsibilities with each other. Once you commit to something you are held to it, but you have the ability to easily move around just by talking to people. Gore refers to this as commitments not assignments.

At Morning Star, employees have what they call CLOUs, which are "colleague letters of understanding." These are essentially peer-to-peer contracts, which employees craft to help describe and commit to Morning Star's success. Although Morning Star was the only company that had this type of peer-to-peer contract-based approach, all of the organizations mentioned earlier share the fact that employees have choice and freedom when it comes to selecting what to work on, but they are also held accountable to the choices they make.

WHO LEADS THE PROJECTS?

There are two approaches that managerless companies typically take. The first is to let leaders or managers emerge organically. This is what happens at Valve—someone inevitably ends up taking the role to guide or help run a team or project. This means that this person has to have followers, so often this ends up being someone who has been at the company a bit longer. If you put a bunch of people on an island someone ends up naturally taking charge, this is the approach that Valve takes.

The second approach that organizations take is one based on peer voting or recognition. It's not too dissimilar to the approach that companies like Valve take, but it's just a bit more structured. When Chuck Carroll, the former CEO of W. L. Gore, retired, his successor was determined by a peer-voting process, Terri Kelly (yes, a female) was voted as the new CEO; she didn't know she would be running the company, and it came as a complete surprise. As she said in an interview with the

Guardian: "We weren't given a list of names—we were free to choose anyone in the company; to my surprise, it was me."

Gore also has separate business units with recognized leaders to help run them.

At GitHub some teams have what they call a PRP or Primarily Responsible Person who helps make sure the team members are accountable for getting done what they need do, this person may also be a coder just like everyone else. However, a PRP doesn't dictate or tell people what to do, they aren't a manager, and instead they can be thought of as more or less facilitators or guides.

Jason Stirman leads people operations at Medium and describes what they have as a loosely based circular hierarchy. Each circle is comprised of a team that has a leader called a *lead link* who is responsible for making sure that the team is getting the work done. So instead of having a pyramid of people there is a pyramid of teams, although the pyramid is pretty flat, perhaps only four levels deep. It is designed to show the relationship between teams so, for example, customer support and service might fall under the product development team.

Supercell takes a similar approach as well. Teams work in groups of around 10 or so developers to create a game. These are then presented to the company to decide if they should be taken to the next level or not. Even the CEO himself can't kill a game if he wanted to, the decisions are all left up to the people who make the games.

Even though some of the companies mentioned earlier might have some form of structure, none of them has an organizational chart. At Morning Star for example, employees would tell you that everyone is a manager.

WHO STEERS THE SHIP?

Without managers guiding the ship who keeps it from crashing into the rocks? Companies have varying approaches here. In organizations like Treehouse, Morning Star, Sun Hydraulics, or Medium the overall corporate direction and mission is guided by the co-founders, CEOs, or executive team of the company (if you're wondering why titles like CFO or CEO might exist to begin with, it's mainly for public facing issues, these titles are not used internally). So an overall direction might be set or guided but how to get there, what products to build, and everything in between is left up to the employee to decide. It's a bit like trying to navigate somewhere. All you know is that you need to get from point A to point B; how to get there is up to you. However, this isn't to say that employees can't help shape the direction as well. Anyone is able to come forward with ideas, which are evaluated. Valve claims its approach is even less guided, according to its employee handbook they make decisions:

> The same way we make other decisions: by waiting for someone to decide that it's the right thing to do, and then letting them recruit other people to work on it with them. We believe in each other to make these decisions, and this faith has proven to be well-founded over and over again.

With the exception of Valve and even perhaps Supercell (both gaming companies), the most common approach has been to have some sort of destination or goal set out for a period of time by "executives" and then employees chart the course to get there.

WHAT ABOUT CAREER PATHS AND CHOICES?

One of the things that virtually all of the companies earlier have in common is the mentality of less supervision, more mentorship and support. Everyone from Medium to Morning Star have mentors or coaches who help employees figure out what projects they should be a part of, what teams they can work with, and what their goals at the company can be. These coaches or mentors can be anyone and everyone but are typically people who have been at the company for a little while and are familiar with the culture and how things get done. New employees at managerless companies are typically a bit off-balance for a few weeks or months while they get a handle on how everyone works but eventually things work out.

WHAT ABOUT RAISES OR PROMOTIONS?

There are a few differences between how companies deal with raises or promotions. There are companies like Sun Hydraulics, which give no bonuses and no perks or Treehouse, which doesn't do any raises with the exception of a 3 percent cost-of-living increase (although it is thinking of implementing a bonus program). Then there are companies like Medium, which has an employee evaluation system where employees are periodically given stock that they can distribute to other employees at the company who they feel are doing a good job (they can't give it to themselves). Morning Star uses an employee-elected "compensation committee," which helps set pay levels for employees after evaluating their performances based on their CLOUs (and some other metrics). Morning Star has no promotions so people get paid more by getting better at their jobs. Shopify, an e-commerce platform, allows employees to assign Unicorns to each other, which is a type of virtual currency. At the end of each month bonuses are given out to employees, which are proportional to the number of Unicorns they have been given by other employees. Valve and GitHub also have a peer-based compensation model.

Overall it's up to your peers to decide how much more money you should get, how much more equity you should have, or what kind of a bonus you should receive. None of the companies profiled have promotions in terms of titles, though.

WHAT HAPPENS IF SOMETHING GOES WRONG?

If there are no managers then who do you go to with a voice for concern about an issue or an employee? What if there is an argument or you don't get along with someone? No surprise, this is also addressed in a communal or peer-based setting. At first employees try to resolve the conflict themselves but if that doesn't work they can either turn to specific conflict resolution committees inside the company or a mediator who can help facilitate a discussion. Sometimes during these conflict resolutions, an employee can be let go.

WHAT MAKES THESE COMPANIES WORK?

Managerless companies are not for everyone. In fact, almost all of the companies mentioned earlier have been candid in publicly stating that. Working in a managerless company definitely takes getting used to and requires a bit of a different mind-set for everyone involved. However, all of the companies mentioned earlier are doing very well in a managerless setting. There are a couple of common threads that make managerless organizations successful but at the core all of the companies have a strong focus on employee happiness.

Transparency

Being open with employees and company information is critical. At Supercell, for example, the CEO sends out an email every morning detailing crucial statistics that would normally be reserved for senior managers. Numbers such as how many new users the company gained, how much money users spent, and total daily active usage are all among the numbers that are shared. Treehouse does this as well and includes numbers such as sign ups and cancellations. It's safe to say that most of the companies have an open door policy, if you want to know about something it's rare that somebody will tell you no.

Freedom with Accountability

Sun Hydraulics, Morning Star, and W. L. Gore offer as much freedom as possible to employees but they are a bit limited in what they can do because they are running manufacturing facilities. However, Automattic, GitHub, Supercell, Valve, and Treehouse have a complete freedom-based approach. Hours worked, days taken off, where you work, and anything else related to how much work you put in are not really paid attention to. Instead, these organizations give employees the freedom to work when they want, how they want, and on what they want to work on. Employees have control but they are also held accountable for the work they do, commitments instead of assignments.

Mentorship and Support

Every company included has a type of mentorship or coaching program. Employees help each other fit in and understand how the company works. These mentors are regular employees just like everyone else and the guidance and support is ongoing. There is always someone to talk to, share feedback with, or get advice from.

Amazing Communication

In this type of an environment clearly having great communication skills is crucial. The nonweb-based companies do this by having employees talk to each other, mixing up the types of employees that work together, limiting manufacturing size, and having employee events; however, they are considering or have been in the process of deploying web-based collaboration platforms. Companies that are already web-based cannot exist without collaboration tools whether they are purchased from vendors or developed in-house. Medium's "high-five" and Shopify's Unicorn and Automattic's P2 are all used in-house. But companies also use things like Google hangouts, internal chat rooms, Skype, and social collaboration software. Employees need to be able to communicate with each other openly and frequently, especially in a distributed team environment.

Long-Term Approach

Creating a managerless company takes time, not months, but often years, especially if the company is larger. It's much easier to build a company from the ground up with this approach than it is to convert an existing one. Some companies have tried the managerless approach unsuccessfully; in fact, there were rumors that a larger search engine company (which starts with "G" and ends with "oogle") tried to go managerless but wasn't able to, so they abandoned their efforts.

Must Reflect Values

Managerless organizations cannot succeed unless these ideas are reflected in their values. Values are more than words—they are the actions that the company takes. The organizations mentioned here didn't become managerless to reflect their values, it's the values that made them go with a managerless structure. Gore values things like creativity, sticking to commitments, and diversity of thought. Supercell values include: minimizing bureaucracy, transparency, celebrating failures, and getting big by thinking small. Sun Hydraulics values having a workforce that is always empowered to help and satisfy the customer, regardless of what its challenge may be. Valve values T-shape people; that is, people who are experts within a specific area yet also skilled in a broad range of other areas. They also value freedom, innovation, and creativity. All of the companies make sure that their values and actions are aligned.

Don't Fear or Punish Failure

None of the companies has a culture of fear or fear of failure. In fact, many actually believe it's okay to fail because it's part of the creative and innovative process. At Valve, for example, when employees can't come to an agreement on something they ship "it" and see who was right, fully aware that there will always be a degree of failure, but as long as they learn from it, it's okay. At Supercell, employees break open a bottle of champagne when they ship a new game or when they kill a game because they view failure as something new that was learned, and that is also worth celebrating.

Understand Employees Have Lives

Managerless companies don't want employees to work 100-hour weeks; in fact, GitHub specifically states that doing something like that is just silly. Employees at Treehouse only work four-day work weeks at 32 hours a week. All of these companies realize that employees are people outside of work with friends and families. In fact, all of these companies typically reference words like *family* and *happiness* when describing their corporate culture. This acknowledgment that employees are humans with spouses, kids, hobbies, and personal interests is extremely important.

Hire the Right People

Perhaps the most important thing that every managerless organization has explicitly stated is the importance in hiring the right people. The right person is basically someone who can work in a managerless environment. Someone who is comfortable with peer recognition, being autonomous, driven, committal, and curious. These companies are also very open in saying that sometimes their environment isn't right for everyone, and that's okay. Managerless organizations require a very high degree of trust among employees to be successful. This is why it's so crucial to make sure the right employees come on board. Because hiring the right person is so important these companies are fine with paying more money for the right person.

THE BENEFITS OF A MANAGERLESS COMPANY

If you were to ask any of these companies why they decided to take a managerless approach they would all list a few things as key benefits.

Innovation

Not only are employees to come up with more and better ideas for existing products or services but they are also able to come up with ideas and opportunities for new things. For example, Gore has a guitar string business, which is doing quite well, yet this was a completely new market that they entered when an employee had a new idea to try out.

Employee Retention

The employee retention and loyalty rates at these companies far surpass what you would find at a traditional organization. People genuinely want to work at these organizations even though some companies like Treehouse don't do raises and companies like Sun Hydraulics don't do bonuses or offer perks. People are there because they are treated like people, because their interests are considered, because they have freedom, and because they are doing things that they want to do.

Faster Decision Making

Without managers the time it takes to make a decision decreases dramatically. Instead of having to get approvals from multiple people, which can take weeks, an employee can make a decision and go with it. This can include everything from making a company purchase for a new computer or desk to bringing on a new employee to the team.

Better Customer Experiences

In managerless organizations employees are empowered to solve customer issues and challenges without always having to escalate them. Sun Hydraulics literally has this idea as a core part of its values. How many times have we been on the phone with a cable company or an airline only to find out that the person on the other end of the line is powerless to help us? We have to either call back or wait for a call or email from a supervisor, which may or may not ever come. It's a horrible customer experience. In managerless organizations the employees help the customers on the spot and that is a powerful thing. The customer experience tends to align with the employee experience and in managerless companies both tend to be quite high.

Eliminate Social Loafing

In a completely autonomous and open environment where peers are evaluating you, it's easy to see which employees contribute and which ones don't. This means there is no room to hide within the organization. If you're a part of the team and aren't pulling your weight, it becomes very clear. Depending on who you ask, this may or may not be a good thing.

The Best People Are Doing the Best Jobs

In managerless companies where employees select what they want to work on, organizations typically hire the best people they can and then those people select the projects or jobs where they can do the best job. This means they care about the work, they enjoy the work, and they get a sense of fulfillment by doing it. The quality of work is higher as is the productivity level of the employee. This doesn't need to be exclusive to managerless companies but it certainly seems to be common among them.

ISSUES WITH MANAGERLESS COMPANIES

The value of a managerless company seems to be quite high, not just for employees but also for the organization as a whole. However, even managerless organizations are not perfect. None of these companies will tell you that they have the perfect model or that their model is scalable for every or any other company. Instead, all of these organizations had to take an approach that made sense for them. Although they don't have managers they do have plenty of differences as mentioned earlier. Still, managerless organizations have their own share of challenges as well.

Informal Hierarchies Still Get Created

In a managerless environment typically people who have been at the organization longer tend to get a bit of informal seniority. This means that as a new employee it becomes hard to get your projects created but it also means that people tend to form cliques; for example, those with more tenure who have already worked together tend to stay together. This can cause tension within the organization.

They Might Not Be as Efficient

Sun Hydraulics admits that as it continues to grow it becomes harder and harder for them to maintain their current structure, especially the cultural aspect. In a blog post written on January 25, 2008 called, "No Titles Except 'Plant' Manager,"[1] Kevin Meyer, a former member of the board of directors at The Association for Manufacturing Excellence, summarized one of the association's meetings where he wrote that a member asked, "If the culture helped them get to $170M, or did it keep them from being at more than $170M?" (today, the market capitalization for Sun Hydraulics is over $1 billion). At Gore, it's not uncommon for the adjustment period to take six months or even a year for new employees. In fact, many new employees are encouraged to spend a part of their first few months just going around meeting and talking to people. These inefficiencies are not blatantly apparent and they might not be that significant to begin with but employees at these companies will tell you that there's probably a more effective way to do things. Still, their approach works for them.

Public Representation May Not Reflect Reality

In a 2011 article for the *Harvard Business Review* by Gary Hamel titled "First, Let's Fire All the Managers," one apparent employee left a comment saying that he saw people get fired for self-managing, that he never saw colleague committees http://www.gsb.stanford.edu/news/research/Building-Organizations-That-Work.html deciding on grievances, that employees were encouraged to "rat each other out" via a "violation box," and that even though people weren't necessarily called *managers* that there were in fact bosses who set rules. At Valve, one employee came out saying, "It is a pseudo-flat structure where, at least in small groups, you're all peers and make decisions together. But the one thing I found out the hard way is that there is actually a hidden layer of powerful management structure in the company and it felt a lot like high school. There are popular kids that have acquired power in the company, then there's the trouble makers, and everyone in between."

Many People Still Want Structure

It turns out that many people still like hierarchies. In a study from Stanford Graduate School of Business, http://www.gsb.stanford.edu/news/research/Building-Organizations-That-Work.html, Professor Larissa Tiedens and Cornell University Assistant Professor Emily Zitek conducted several interesting experiments. In one experiment participants were shown several different diagrams, which each contained the names of seven men. One diagram showed the men listed in a hierarchy, another showed them linked in a circle, and a third showed them "chunked" into random groups without any sign of hierarchical structure. Respondents were asked to reproduce the diagrams and once they successfully did, the experiment was over. The participants learned the hierarchy diagram the fastest. In total, five experiments were conducted that compared hierarchies versus more flat structures. An article published by Susan H. Greenberg on the Stanford Graduate School of Businessblog on August 1, 2012 called, "Building Organizations That Work"[2] summarized the findings of the report:

> [H]ierarchies are easier for people to grasp than egalitarian relationships because their asymmetries create "end points" that facilitate memorization; they are predictable; and they are familiar, beginning with our very first social interaction—the parent-child relationship.
>
> Professor Tiedens, one of the authors of the study said, "Equality can be messy, and hierarchy is conceptually cleaner."
>
> The article continues: "Tiedens believes the most successful organizations are those that achieve a balance between hierarchy and equality."

IS THIS RIGHT FOR YOU?

What we can tell from all of this is that there certainly is a place for managerless companies. In fact, there are several very successful companies that adopt this approach. This doesn't mean it's for everyone. There are no perfect companies and there are pros and cons to any type of corporate structure that an organization goes after. Keep in mind that the largest managerless company featured here is W. L. Gore with around 10,000 employees, with Sun Hydraulics in second with around 2,500 employees. All the other companies are just under 1,000 employees, with many of them at a few hundred or lower.

A managerless approach may be the best solution for your company or it may not be. However, the goal of exploring this is to show that it is indeed possible. We need fewer people focusing on command and control, hierarchy, and supervision and more people focused on creating followers, challenging assumptions, influencing, mentoring, supporting, and allowing for freedom and flexibility. You can call them managers, leaders, facilitators or anything else you want to call them, but again that's irrelevant.

According to the previously mentioned article published by Stanford, just because participants found hierarchies easier for people to understand doesn't mean that,

> [W]e should abandon the idea of equality in favor of a rigid chain of command; it just means that organizations keen on eliminating or minimizing hierarchy, as seems to be the trend, should be prepared to replace it with something else. Just getting rid of the organizational chart can create problems. People often think equality is a natural state that doesn't have to be managed, but it does. It's harder for people to understand and learn an egalitarian structure. So you need more clarity in other structural variables, like really clear job titles, for instance. Such titles need not delineate a pecking order; instead of names like "manager," "director," or "associate," companies could just make the titles extremely specific, such as "writer in charge of advertising copy" or "coordinator of sustainability activities."

Organizations are encouraged to experiment and try new approaches when it comes to management, the findings might be surprising, and there's really only one way to tell if this approach is indeed right for your organization. It's hard to claim that managerless organizations are the way of the future because the reality is that for most companies in the world that just isn't true. It's tough to imagine going into an organization with tens of thousands or hundreds of thousands of employees and making this change. Although managerless organizations might not become the majority, organizations that believe in a new way of "managing" will become the majority.

To help give you a comparison of how a traditional company and a managerless company handle and deal with various issues you can look at Figure 7.1. There are clear and distinct differences between everything from how employees are hired or fired to how issues or conflicts within the organization are addressed and resolved.

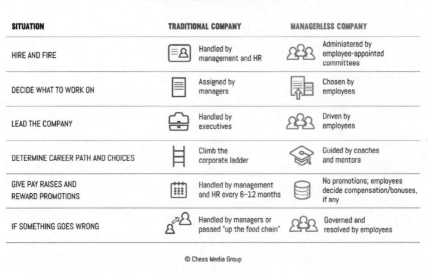

THE MANAGERLESS COMPANY

SITUATION	TRADITIONAL COMPANY	MANAGERLESS COMPANY
HIRE AND FIRE	Handled by management and HR	Administered by employee-appointed committees
DECIDE WHAT TO WORK ON	Assigned by managers	Chosen by employees
LEAD THE COMPANY	Handled by executives	Driven by employees
DETERMINE CAREER PATH AND CHOICES	Climb the corporate ladder	Guided by coaches and mentors
GIVE PAY RAISES AND REWARD PROMOTIONS	Handled by management and HR every 6–12 months	No promotions; employees decide compensation/bonuses, if any
IF SOMETHING GOES WRONG	Handled by managers or passed "up the food chain"	Governed and resolved by employees

© Chess Media Group

FIGURE 7.1   The Managerless Company

CHAPTER **8**

The Organization of Today

Around 100 to 150 years ago many people worked for themselves as blacksmiths, carpenters, masons, or one of the many other jobs around at that time. Education also wasn't the primary driver for getting a job, schooling for many jobs was actually irrelevant. What was important was the ability to get an apprenticeship where you can learn skills and get training. Today education takes precedence. An entire book could easily be written about (and many have) the issues and challenges with our present-day education system and why organizations are so focused on hiring people who earned a piece of paper from a university, but that's a whole separate topic. For the most part, organizations as we know them today started growing around the time Henry Ford started his automotive empire close to 100 years ago. This is what many consider to be the creation of a true company.

Organizations were not created with the idea of change and adaptability in mind. Instead they were created to be immovable fortresses, impenetrable by any force or any competitor. After all, it was not possible to predict the changes that we see today nor the continued increase in the rate of change that is taking our organizations into the future. Organizations were not constructed in an adaptable way, so they tend to break apart or fracture in a rapidly changing world. Companies like Blockbuster, Loehmann's, Borders, Research in Motion, and others are examples of companies that have tried and failed to adapt—too little too late.

Keep in mind that organizations were created for the primary purpose of making money; that was and still remains their primary goal (at least for most companies). Employees were viewed as fuel to help the machine keep running. This is the mentality and the idea that has carried over into many of our organizations today. It's reflected in corporate cultures, management practices, the way employees feel, and how things get done. These are the types of companies that are in danger regardless of how big or small they are.

We have to consider a few things when thinking about the future organization.

JOB SECURITY ISN'T SO SECURE

The traditional assumption of a larger organization was that it was safer because it offered job security. However, if we look at what has happened to many organizations over the past few years we quickly realize that the notion of job security isn't so secure. As I'm writing this, Merck is laying off 8,500 workers, Alitalia (the national airline of Italy) is proposing to lay off 2,000 workers, BlackBerry is cutting around 5,000, Safeway is laying off around 6,000 (through their Dominick's chain), Kellogg's is cutting more than 2,000, Thomson Reuters is cutting 4,500, Cisco is cutting around 4,000, EADS is cutting up to 6,000, and this list can go on and on—and this was just in the past month! The trend isn't just with large companies either. If you pay a visit to Dailyjobcuts.com you can see this trend happening around the world at companies of all sizes, but the larger impacts are primarily felt by larger companies. That's because when organizations grow to such a large scale and size the only way to have a dramatic impact on the bottom line is to make big sweeping cuts and this happens often. So the idea of working at an established company for job security is becoming less and less true.

The average life expectancy of an organization on the S&P 500 used to be 75 years. Today that number has plummeted to just around 15 years and appears to keep shrinking. In fact, according to Clayton Christensen's research firm Innosight, by 2027, 75 percent of the S&P 500 are going to be replaced.

Figure 8.1 paints a visual picture of what is happening.

Note that the number of publicly traded companies overall (as measured by the Wilshire 5000 Index) decreased from 5,672 companies in 2002 to 3,687 companies in 2012. This includes companies that were acquired, delisted, merged, have gone private, or have gone bust. Meanwhile the number of IPOs over the past four years has averaged at just 118.

This isn't about advocating jumping ship and joining a small three-person start-up, though. It's simply to point out that the notion of

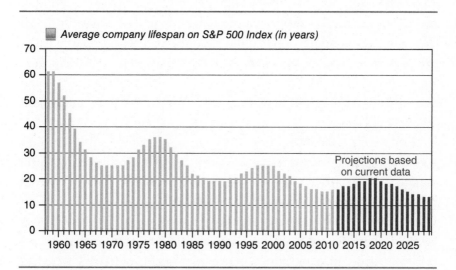

FIGURE 8.1   Average Company Lifespan on S&P 500 Index (in Years)

Source: Innosight.

job security is a myth. As a result, it changes the way new and current employees think about and react to work.

LOYALTIES HAVE SHIFTED

Thomas Friel[1] is the former CEO of Heidrick & Struggles, a global executive search firm that was at one point ranked by the *Wall Street Journal* as the top executive search firm in the world. Perhaps the most famous placement by Heidrick & Struggles was the CEO of Google, Eric Schmidt in 2004. Friel has since retired, but during a recent conversation we discussed how the employee and employer relationship is changing.

Sixty-plus years ago there was an implicit contract between employees and employers. Employees would commit to working at companies and those companies would take care of the employees for life. In fact, lifetime (or very long term) employment was standard. Then, when employees would retire they would get pensions. Employees didn't really think about leaving companies unless they were either fired or if the company closed down. Happiness, doing challenging work, creativity, innovation, and engagement weren't primary concerns back then. Employees had a virtually endless threshold as far as what they "would be willing to take" or put up with at work. They were there to do a job and they did it.

Today this relationship has changed dramatically. Employees now stay at companies for around four years and lifetime or even long-term employment is virtually unheard of, as are pensions. Today's loyalties have shifted away from companies toward managers, teams, or projects. If we work with people we really like and those people switch companies we may follow them if there is an opportunity for us to do so. Today we give some of our time and attention to employers but once we start to feel unhappy we start looking for something better. Our threshold of what we are willing to put up with has dramatically shrunk and we are quick to turn to other opportunities. The 2013 Kelly Global Workplace Index report, called "Employee Engagement and Retention,"[2] which surveyed

120,000 employees in 31 countries, found that in the United States 42 percent of respondents changed jobs in the past year. In Australia this number was 62 percent, in the United Kingdom 50 percent, Canada 49 percent, and in China 34 percent.

IT'S NO LONGER JUST ABOUT MONEY

Most companies have traditionally used money as a way to attract and retain top talent. The larger the organization, the more money it could usually afford to pay employees and allocate for other resources. This means that the top talent typically went to larger organizations because they could pay more. However, what good is that money when the future workforce is starting to prioritize other things ahead of higher salaries? As discussed earlier, the future employee wants a flexible work environment, career path opportunities, the chance to do meaningful work, and several other things aside from just getting a paycheck. This means that many organizations can't leverage their single greatest resource to help them, cash.

SELF-STARTER OPPORTUNITIES

Technology costs are going down and the number of methods and ease of raising money today are going up. Sites such as Gofundme, Kickstarter, Indiegogo, and dozens of others are allowing people to raise cash for their ideas or projects; billions of dollars have already been raised on these sites. There are several marketplaces now such as Elance-oDesk where people can build their own businesses and work as freelancers. Uber and Lyft allow almost anyone with a car to make $35 an hour ($75,000 a year) by driving people around and Task Rabbit allows you to hire anyone to help with things you might need to get done, such as painting a house (which is what I used them for) or delivering groceries. The point is that working for a company isn't the only way to make money anymore. More and more alternatives are emerging that allow smart people to grow and build a business and the incentive to do so is actually quite high.

SMALLER GROWING COMPANIES

Many people are rapidly gravitating toward either creating or working for start-ups or more forward thinking companies. Take a look at companies such as Box, Uber, Square, Fitbit, and the many others out there that are challenging and disrupting traditional markets such as transportation, banking and payments, health and wellness, and even enterprise software. Many of these smaller and rapidly growing organizations cater to the key principles of the future employee mentioned in the first section of the book, which means that the competition for larger organizations to attract and retain top talent is extremely fierce. These companies aren't successful just because they are smaller; they are successful because they are able to bring in the best talent. It's no surprise that many of these organizations were started and are primarily staffed by millennials.

GROWING UP SKEPTICAL

Many millennials have seen their parents and parents, friends get laid off from jobs or talk about how unhappy they were at work, which already puts a negative impression in their minds. I saw my mom go through a career change from being a program manager at a large organization to going back to school to become a marriage and family therapist. She was not happy at her previous company and had to do something else. This is quite common among the younger generation and so the future workforce is already quite skeptical about working for established large organizations.

I don't want to sound overly negative here, though. There are still some fantastic larger organizations that are growing today. Companies like Apple or Google are among the first that come to mind.

Many larger organizations also still do have their advantages such as career growth opportunities, the ability to work in many countries around the world, great benefit packages, compensation for continued education, and brand name recognition. However, what is happening is that there's a battle for talent taking place and the only way any type of organization is going to win is by becoming the "future company."

The point is that organizations of all shapes and sizes need to adapt. The advantage that many of the newer or smaller companies have is that they can change quickly. Many companies have already been built from the ground up with the future employee in mind. It's much easier to build something from scratch than it is to tear down a large structure and rebuild. The larger and older organizations have to rebuild and change long-standing ideas, approaches, and strategies. However, even the smaller and newer companies run the risk of turning back the hands of time while forgetting to focus on the future employee.

The idea of these massive companies that we have today is a fairly new concept and idea. In about a century we went from working individuals to these behemoth organizations who employ tens of thousands or hundreds of thousands of people around the world. These companies grew out of a desire to make more profits; more profits means more people. But nothing can keep growing forever, which begs the question, "How much larger can some of these organizations possibly get?" Just between you and me, I'm not so sure that some of these organizations were ever meant to get to be as big as they are today. Although I do believe that larger organizations are primarily in jeopardy, it's actually any organization that operates based on concepts from the past instead of adapting to the future that is at risk. We just happen to see this type of legacy mentality more often in larger, more established companies. The primary reason why so many companies today are in jeopardy is because—quite frankly—future employees just won't want to work there.

CHAPTER 9

Fourteen Principles of the Future Organization

So what does the future organization look like? There are 14 principles of the future organization, as shown on Figure 9.1.

The future organization will:

- Have employees work in globally distributed yet smaller teams.
- Become intrapreneurial.
- Create a connected workforce.
- Operate like a smaller company.
- Focus on creating a place of "want" instead of a place of "need."
- Adapt to change faster.
- Innovate anywhere, all the time.
- Build ecosystems.
- Run in the cloud.
- See more women in senior management roles.
- Be "flatter."
- Tell stories.
- Democratize learning.
- Shift from profit to prosperity.
- Adapt to the future employee and the future manager.
- Become globally distributed with smaller teams.

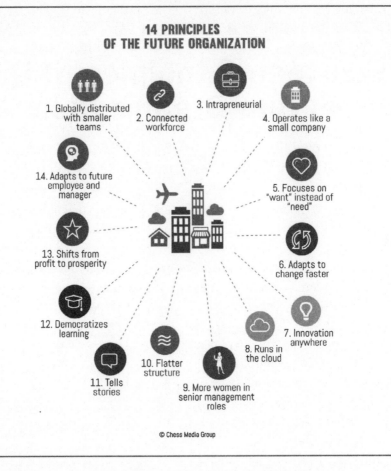

**14 PRINCIPLES
OF THE FUTURE ORGANIZATION**

1. Globally distributed with smaller teams

2. Connected workforce

3. Intrapreneurial

4. Operates like a small company

14. Adapts to future employee and manager

5. Focuses on "want" instead of "need"

13. Shifts from profit to prosperity

6. Adapts to change faster

12. Democratizes learning

7. Innovation anywhere

8. Runs in the cloud

10. Flatter structure

11. Tells stories

9. More women in senior management roles

© Chess Media Group

FIGURE 9.1   Fourteen Principles of the Future Organization

It's hard to imagine today's companies continuing to operate the way they are. They are spreading out all over the world and now that we can get our jobs done simply by connecting to the Internet we can have offices anywhere. It's not uncommon for some organizations to have one or two employees working from home in remote parts of the world just so that they can say they have an office in that location. Although companies are spreading out all over the world they are leveraging technology to stay connected and collaborative. There are many benefits to having a distributed company, but perhaps the most significant is the ability to tap into a global talent pool.

Employees can be hired from every corner of the world whether they be in San Francisco, Mumbai, Melbourne, or Beijing. Globally distributed organizations can hire top talent anywhere they find it. These types of diverse workforces bring with them different ideas, perspectives, and approaches to work, which means innovation. In a traditional work environment where homogeneity was the standard, this type of diversity is the new normal. This means that the future organization will come to rely on the freelancer economy for talent. This can either be done by tapping into existing marketplaces and platforms that already exist or by organizations creating their own environments where employees can pick the projects they want to work on and then transition once those are completed. This will lead to a much more dynamic and adaptable workplace but the idea of employees only working for one company, for one manager, or on one project is losing steam. Again, this is especially relevant when considering that the average U.S. employee tenure is 4.6 years and 2.3 years for employees between the ages of 20 to 34.[1]

Other benefits of smaller and globally distributed teams also exist, such as the ability to enter new markets with local employees who understand the local culture and customs, continuous work around the clock (when San Francisco is sleeping London is working), and the ability to keep things moving, and workplace flexibility. These teams cannot be supported and connected without the right tools to enable them to work.

Jeff Bezos, the founder and CEO of Amazon, famously created the "two-pizza rule," which means that if a team couldn't be fed with two pizzas, then it was too big. The idea is that the more people you have working on a project together the more chaotic things can get. Then there's a tendency for people to just agree with each other, which means that different opinions and ideas don't get voiced. Smaller teams can make decisions quicker and it's much easier for them to stay on the same page. This doesn't mean that small teams can't be tapped into the collective intelligence of the company or other teams, though.

There might be something to this. Gallup's 2013 report called "State of the American Workplace"[2] found that the smallest companies have the most engaged employees. According to Gallup, 42 percent of employees working at companies of 10 and fewer employees reported that they were engaged at work. Compare this with around the 30 percent number, which is found at larger companies. Gallup also found that 44 percent of employees work at companies with more than 1,000 employees and only 9 percent of workers in the United States work at smaller companies. This doesn't mean that smaller companies have to be better than larger companies but data suggests that smaller teams can be more efficient and effective.

THE RINGELMANN EFFECT

The Ringelmann effect is a fascinating tendency for individual members to become less productive as the size of the group increases. We have all experienced this either in college when working on team projects where someone slacks off or in the corporate setting where we feel other members don't pull their weight. This theory has been tested repeatedly and proven to be true. Ringelmann first ran this experiment around 100 years ago by asking volunteers to pull on a rope. He found that when one person is pulling on the rope they give 100 percent effort but as more people are added the individual effort goes down largely because of the challenge of extracting individual contributions and performance. In the 1970s Alan Ingham replicated this experiment with rope pulling and clapping and shouting experiments. He came up with the concept of *social loafing* where people deliberately exhibit less effort as the group increases. The theory was that this happens because the contributors don't feel like their efforts will really make a difference to the group or be recognized.

Collectively, research shows that larger teams don't do as well for three reasons: the loss of individual motivation, challenges in coordination, and what UC San Diego Professor Jennifer Mueller calls *relational loss*, which is where individuals feels as though the amount of support they get decreases as the size of the team increases.

Finally, we have another interesting experiment conducted by three professors from UCLA, Penn State, and Chapel Hill. Professors Staats, Milkman, and Fox[3] asked two sets of teams to put together a structure made out of LEGO bricks. Teams were broken up into either two or four people. On average two person teams took 36 minutes to put together the LEGO structure and the teams of four people took 56 minutes to put together the LEGO structure.

Several strategies exist to counter this, such as increasing the ability to identify individual contributions and setting clear goals. Collaboration technologies can really help here as they allow employees to share and get recognized for their individual contributions while getting visibility into how their efforts impact the greater team and company.

Supercell is a 100-person game company based in Finland. The CEO, Ilkka Paananen, calls himself the world's least powerful CEO. The company is valued at around $3 billion and makes more than $2.5 million every single day. What's particularly fascinating about Supercell is that it is much smaller than the other gaming companies out there, which have several times the number of employees that Supercell has. The structure at Supercell is also quite unique as the company is organized as a set of small independent teams or "cells," which are given complete autonomy over what they work on, how they organize themselves, what ideas get prioritized, and the products or games that are created. Today, Supercell is considered to be one of the hottest gaming start-ups in the world by *Business Insider*.

The Ringlemann effect is a fascinating topic that I encourage everyone to read more about. It's no wonder the Jeff Bezos's two-pizza rule makes so much sense. The research clearly suggests that smaller distributed teams are the way to go. In most organizations today, teams can easily reach several dozens of people. I have been on several conference calls with client teams where the number of people easily reached 35 to 40 people and most of them end up staying quiet the entire time.

Connecting people and building a network is certainly valuable but when it comes to the future organization, the teams themselves should be smaller and more distributed.

INTRAPRENEURIAL

Intrapreneurial is the concept of being an entrepreneur while working inside an organization and it will be important for the future organization. When we think of an entrepreneur we usually think of someone who has an idea for a business, product, or service and then turns that idea into a reality. Sergey Brin and Larry Page, Steve Jobs, Nolan Bushnell, Bill Gates, Mark Zuckerberg, and Richard Branson are all well-known entrepreneurs. The term first appeared almost 300 years ago but was coined by either French economist Jean-Baptiste Say or Irish-French Economist Richard Cantillon (depending on which version of history you subscribe to). Interestingly, the word *entrepreneur* has gone through several evolutions of definitions starting with Richard Cantillon in 1734, who called entrepreneurs "non-fixed income earners who pay known costs of production but earn uncertain incomes" to Ronald May who defined it as "someone who commercializes his or her innovation."

Entrepreneurs don't work for other people, they "do their own thing," when they have an idea they are able to act on it to help make it a reality. The idea of an intrapraneur takes this idea and brings it inside organizations.

LinkedIn, the business social network, has around 5,000 employees and in 2014 crossed the 300-million user mark. Recently it launched its own internal incubator aptly called "[in]cubator" to help turn its employees into intrapreneurs. Employees pitch their ideas and raise funding the same way they would if they were entrepreneurs not employed by LinkedIn trying to get money from venture capitalists. Thus far five projects have been approved with many more expected to roll out in the future.

The concept of being intrapreneurial allows employees within the organization to come up with and make their ideas happen. It's about innovation and creativity, which is the lifeblood of most organizations today.

A 2013 study by Millennial Branding and American Express called "Gen Y Workplace Expectations,"[4] found that 58 percent of managers are either very or extremely willing to support the entrepreneur endeavors of millennials. Remember that millennials are going to be 50 percent of the workforce by 2020 and 75 percent of the workforce by 2025, so this is an important area for organizations to focus on. The study also found that almost half (46 percent) of millennial employees are interested in entrepreneurial endeavors.

There are many examples of innovative products, which came from intrapreneurs. Google's Gmail, Adsense, and Google News were all products created by the famous 20-percent time rule where employees can spend 20 percent of their time working on projects that interest them. Post-its, made famous by 3M, is another example of where an intrapreneur had an idea and thanks to 3M's "permitted bootlegging" policy (where employees can spend 10 percent to 15 percent of time working on "pet" projects) was able to run with it and eventually make it quite successful. Dreamworks Animation, the 2,000-plus person company with hits like *Shrek, Rise of the Guardians, Antz*, and others, allows any employee to pitch a movie idea to members of the executive team and even offers workshops and mentoring on how to make this pitch successful. Virgin Atlantic is another interesting and compelling example of the power of intrapreneurship. Ten years ago, Virgin hired several top design firms to help out with some design specifications for its first-class cabins and the private sleeper suites it wanted to create. Joe Ferry, who is now the head of design at Virgin, volunteered to help and was able to solve the design problem that none of the top design firms could.

Richard Branson, the founder of the Virgin Group of more than 400 companies, asks an interesting question in an article he wrote on

January 31, 2011 for *Entrepreneur Magazine* called, "Richard Branson on Intrapreneurs."[5] In the article he asks: "What if CEO stood for 'chief enabling officer'? What if that CEO's primary role were to nurture a breed of intrapreneurs who would grow into tomorrow's entrepreneurs?"

In that same article he commented on entering the mobile phone market by saying:

> [W]e had no experience, so we looked for our rivals' best managers, hired them away, took off their ties and gave them the freedom to set up their own ventures within the Virgin Group. Tom Alexander in the U.K., Dan Schulman in the U.S. and Andrew Black in Canada have all done this with great success, aggressively taking Virgin companies in new and unexpected directions.

The future organization must enable, support, and help create intrapreneurs. These are the employees who will create new products, come up with new ideas, develop new strategies, and provide that unique competitive advantage. At an innovation conference I attended in early 2014 their CTO Padmasree Warrior mentioned that engineers are given the freedom to start their own companies, sometimes with the support of Cisco. If Cisco sees that the companies have potential or are working on something interesting then they try to buy them back. This is a fantastic example of encouraging intrapreneurs. Research shows that this type of an environment is also very much welcomed by the future employee. Not everyone wants to be an entrepreneur or an intrapreneur and that's fine, the same way that not every employee will want to work remotely. The important thing here for the future organization is to allow and support those employees who do want to take this path. There must be a way for these employees to come forward with ideas and to move forward with them because if they don't share them with their current employer, chances are they will share them with their next employer.

CONNECTED WORKFORCE

When it comes to the future of work and the future organization, it's crucial that employees and information be connected to each other anytime, anywhere, and on any device. Employees are no longer working from one office, in one location, with one department, or in one time zone. Every employee is now a global worker. This isn't just about crossing boundaries, it's about tearing them out of the walls and getting rid of them altogether.

It seems a bit silly to try to explain why connecting employees is so crucial, yet for some reason many organizations don't do it.

In my previous book, *The Collaborative Organization*, I laid out a comprehensive strategic framework for how to go about building this type of an organization, focused on collaboration. I explored everything from developing use cases and selecting technologies to marketing these efforts, creating teams, and building a long-term sustainable strategy. It's a much more strategic approach with models and frameworks so if you're interested in that then I recommend you check out that book.

Whether employees are on a mobile device in a cab, on a laptop in a café, or sitting on a couch at home using a tablet, they must always be able to "connect to work." Not only is this something that the future employee will expect, it's something that the future organization must focus on to thrive.

A connected workforce speeds up decision making, reduces content duplication, improves organizational alignment, improves innovation, improves communication and collaboration, and makes it easier for employees to get work done.

In my presentations at conferences I like to use an analogy. We never know what tomorrow is going to bring. In fact, the only thing we can be certain of is that there is always uncertainty. So, how do organizations want to approach that type of an environment where they never know what tomorrow will bring? Organizations can either approach uncertainty in a fragmented and siloed way (which many do today), or they can approach that uncertainty in a connected way, where all the employees can come together to help solve problems and identify opportunities.

Connecting your workforce relies on technology as the enabler, but it also centers on the new behaviors that employees are bringing into the workforce and the new approaches that managers and leaders must adapt to help support a connected workforce.

OPERATE LIKE A SMALL COMPANY

If you take a look at many smaller companies you will notice that they tend to do things a bit differently. They make decisions quicker, they try and experiment with new ideas, they don't focus as much on hierarchies, and for the most part they seem to be more adaptable and agile than larger monster organizations.

I know several people who work for larger organizations who love their jobs and I myself am a fan of many large organizations out there. The truth is it's hard to talk about why larger organizations should operate more like smaller organizations without ending up verbally bashing larger entities or making this a debate about the big company versus the small company. That's really not what my intention is here. Instead, I simply want to point out that due to the many changes mentioned earlier in this book, it's becoming increasingly important for larger established organizations to rethink how they operate. It's just as important, however, for smaller and mid-size companies to keep pace as well.

In his book *David and Goliath*, Malcolm Gladwell challenges the common idea that Goliath should have beaten David. Malcolm points out that everyone thought Goliath should have won because he was bigger and stronger (aka large corporations today). However, perhaps David (aka the smaller company) actually had the advantage. He was faster, more flexible and agile, and smarter than Goliath was.

Today there is a bit of a paradox for many organizations. As organizations grow so does their complexity, which results in their becoming slower and less nimble or agile. In other words, the larger an organization gets the slower it moves. However, organizations also realize that the world is changing faster than it ever has before. So here we have a situation in which organizations are making themselves slower and less adaptable when they know that the future of work is about being more adaptable and nimble. The challenge that many organizations have is that they want to keep growing and becoming more complex while simultaneously becoming more agile and adaptable. To give you an analogy, it's like trying to lose weight while consuming many more calories. There are a few possible scenarios for what can happen.

The first is that some organizations will become too big or profitable to fail (or at least that's what they think). These are organizations that have so much money, so many assets, so many customers, and are so profitable that they don't see a need to do anything differently. This is certainly possible but whether it is probable remains to be seen.

The second is that smaller, newer, and more nimble incumbents will continuously challenge and displace their larger counterparts. We see this disruption happening everywhere. Take a look at how Box is challenging companies like Oracle, Netflix taking down Blockbuster, Square putting pressure on financial services and payment companies, Uber disrupting transportation services, and how Spotify is changing the music industry. Larger organizations are quickly trying to acquire and gobble up these smaller disruptors. These are just a few examples, but they can be found everywhere.

The third is that organizations split into more manageable pieces to enable themselves to be adaptable, nimble, and agile. Instead of amassing themselves into larger entities they will instead distribute themselves to be able to collectively move faster. This is another place where the freelancer economy can play a crucial role.

It still remains to be seen whether organizations can become too profitable to fail or whether organizations must break off into smaller more manageable pieces. One thing appears to be true—the future organization must focus on being more like David and less like Goliath.

As we saw in the Jeff Bezos example, bigger isn't necessarily better. In fact, research from CYBAEA[6] actually found that the larger an organization is, the less productive it is.

If you recall, earlier I mentioned how by 2027, 75 percent of the S&P 500 may be replaced and CYBAEA may help point out why; it calls it the 3/2 rule. When you triple the number of employees you halve their productivity or, when you increase the number of employees by 10 percent, productivity falls by 6.3 percent. As far as what causes this, there is no definitive proven answer. However, this also correlates with what was explored in the Ringlemann effect hinting at issues of social loafing, communication, collaboration, and coordination. Regardless, the numbers are definitely a wake-up call. The original analysis was done in 2006 on S&P 500 companies and was redone again in 2010,[7] focusing on the FTSE 100, the London Stock Exchange. The results were similar but not as extreme. CYBAEA found that FTSE 100 companies with 10 times the number of employees generated one-fourth of the productivity as their smaller competitors.

Now this isn't meant to paint every large organization with the same brush, we are certainly speaking in broad terms here, but the trend is real and the data certainly seems to support it.

The future of many large organizations is still up in the air but when looking at some organizations with tens of thousands or hundreds of thousands of employees one can't help but wonder if they wouldn't be more effective to split up into smaller entities instead of remaining as behemoths.

When most people think of working for a smaller company, a few benefits or advantages tend to come to mind:

- Decisions are made faster.
- The company as a whole can be more nimble.
- There is room for out-of-the-box thinking and experimentation.
- Employees have flexibility with their roles, functions, and work styles.

- Alignment is typically clearer.
- Successes are more recognizable and visible.
- There is better communication and collaboration.

Often these are the very things missing from larger organizations. In fact, we see many large organizations (some mentioned in this book) trying to bring in the small company culture.

FOCUS ON "WANT" INSTEAD OF "NEED"

Needing something is about requiring it because "it" is essential or important, such as air or food. Wanting something is about wishing for or desiring "it" but not necessarily because it is essential, such as a nice car or a five-course meal at a fancy restaurant. Employees used to take jobs because they needed them, they needed the money to pay bills and support their families, this was crucial.

Today the attitude of employees is dramatically shifting. At the end of 2013 the unemployment rate for millennials was somewhere around 16.2 percent despite the fact that millennials are often said to be the most educated generation in history. Sadly this generation also carries the largest amount of debt. The changing attitude can be adequately described in a great *New York Times* article published on November 30, 2013 titled "Millennial Searchers."[8] In it the authors write:

Millennials appear to be more interested in living lives defined by meaning than by what some would call happiness. They report being less focused on financial success than they are on making a difference. A 2011 report commissioned by the Career Advisory Board and conducted by Harris Interactive, found that the No. 1 factor that young adults ages 21 to 31 wanted in a successful career was a sense of meaning. Though their managers, according to the study, continue to think that millennials are primarily motivated by money, nearly three-quarters of the young adults surveyed said that "meaningful work" was among the three most important factors defining career success.

Many organizations today still look to attract and retain top talent assuming that the talent needs the company more than the company needs the talent. Dan Pink said it best, "Today, talented people need organizations less than organizations need talented people." Many companies still focus on competitive salaries and great benefits packages when that's not what the future employee prioritizes anymore.

Think of it like this: If you dramatically cut the salaries of your employees or even stopped paying them altogether, would any of them come back to the office tomorrow? Why? What is it that keeps the passionate and engaged employees coming back? I'm willing to bet it's not the money.

Organizations of the future must recognize that the priorities of the future employees have shifted dramatically and they are no longer taking jobs and working for companies because they need to but because they want to. This shift in mind-set will dramatically change how organizations hire, who they hire, and how they grow. This is often an area that many organizations overlook.

Netflix has more than 2,000 employees and has done an excellent job of focusing on creating a place where people work because they want to, not just because they need to. Netflix posted a 126-slide presentation on Slideshare about its corporate culture, which clearly laid out the types of employees it wants, what it values, and why employees want to work there.

In the presentation Netflix's CEO Reed Hastings outlines one of its core beliefs—freedom. He says, "Responsible people thrive on freedom, and are worthy of freedom." Whereas most organizations relinquish freedom as they grow, Netflix actually increases employee freedom with growth. It does this because (as is said in the presentation) as organizations grow so does the complexity, rules are put in place to help manage complexity and in the end force the organization to remain rigid and focused on short-term profits; then, when the market shifts, the organization isn't able to adapt and thus becomes irrelevant. Flexibility is more important than efficiency in the long term.

Netflix doesn't track the number of hours that an employee works per day, has an unlimited vacation policy, has no dress code, and its policy around expenses and gifts is five words long, "Act in Netflix's best interest." Netflix also has an interesting approach to compensation. It would rather pay more for one excellent employee than pay that amount or less for two adequate employees. Instead of offering bonuses, free stock options, or any type of philanthropic matching it just gives people larger salaries and lets them decide what to do with the money. It's important to note that although Netflix employees are also compensated well, their compensation ranks number six on their list of seven aspects of their culture behind things such as high performance, values, freedom and responsibility, and others.

Netflix's transparency in how it works, what it values, how it pays, and what it expects is part of what makes it a company where people work because they want to not because they need to—the pay is the icing on the cake.

ADAPTS TO CHANGE FASTER

Adapting to change has long been known to be a crucial component for the success of any organization. However, adapting to change meant taking a few years to see what everyone else was doing and then gradually following behind. Most organizations assume that adapting to change is akin to being a late follower. However, today "late follower, late majority, or laggard" means "out of business."

This isn't just about adapting to change, it's about adapting to change at a faster pace. In 2011 the Economist Group surveyed 390 executives around the world and found that nearly half (48 percent) say their decision-making times have increased. This is a troubling statistic.

We've seen how many organizations in the S&P 500 are being displaced at a rapid pace, but we are also seeing a continued increased rate of change in many areas. Technology is one of them. A few years ago entire buildings were devoted to housing the computing power that each and every one of us now has in our pockets in the form of our cell phone.

When new technologies or ideas were introduced around 100 years ago, organizations could wait a few years before making those changes themselves. Today, waiting a few years is the equivalent to waiting a decade or more. The market penetration of things like the Internet, smartphones, tablets, and wearable technologies is far surpassing anything we had in the past. This is only increasing, according to the World Intellectual Property Organization (WIPO). Patent applications have been increasing steadily over the past few years at a rate of between 7 and 10 percent each year. The number of patents that have been granted worldwide has averaged double-digit growth rates since 2010 at almost 12 percent.

However, it's not just new technologies that are rapidly entering our organizations, it's also new ideas about work, such as flexible work environments, managers who follow from the front, and organizations focused on collaboration instead of competition.

Future organizations are going to become much more adaptable to the changes that are happening around the world of work and the organizations that don't adapt quickly won't succeed. We already see this happening in the S&P 500, but consider the choices that the future employees are going to make as they graduate college and join companies. Will they work for organizations adapting to new expectations and technologies or those that are not? Top talent will go with the "faster" adaptive organizations.

INNOVATION FROM ANYWHERE, ALL THE TIME, AND CREATING ECOSYSTEMS

In a 2013 report called "Unleashing the Power of Innovation,"[9] PwC surveyed 246 CEOs in North and South America, Europe, Asia Pacific, and the Middle East. It found that 97 percent of CEOs see innovation as a top priority for their business.

GE did some interesting research around this issue in its 2013 Innovation Barometer, which surveyed more than 3,000 executives in 25 countries. Based on their averages, 87 percent of the respondents say that their organizations can be more successful with innovation through partnerships instead of going at it alone.

New ideas for products and services used to come from specific teams within organizations such as research and development (R&D) and for many companies this is still true today. Although there are now dozens of innovation theories and processes that have been developed, the traditional template looks something like this. Come up with an idea, create a proof of concept or prototype to test it out, do the actual testing, and if all goes well then start creating the product (or service) and marketing it. The problem with relying on a team or small group of people to come up with ideas is that you're limiting the number and quality of potential innovative ideas. Why not tap into a much broader ecosystem to help with innovation? The future organization must develop "innovation ecosystems."

The problem, at least internally, is that many organizations' failure is still punished, so you can imagine the reluctance of employees to contribute ideas to anything.

The future organization enables innovation to come from anywhere and at anytime and it doesn't treat failure as some sort of disease that must be cured. For the future organization innovation can come from five places: employees, customers, partners, the general public, or from competitors. Often the term *open innovation* is used to describe the approach to innovation from either external or internal contributors. Innovations can came in the form of products, cost-cutting ideas, marketing programs, service offerings, better customer experience, or anything else. Innovation must extend far beyond a group of people or a team and digital technologies are helping make that happen.

Employee-Driven Innovation

Employees are the most valuable asset that any organization has; they service customers, build products, market those products, develop services, and keep the organization running. Many of these same employees also have ideas on how to improve products or services that the company creates yet they have no way of sharing or realizing those ideas. The smart companies understand the value in employee innovation.

At Toyota factories around the world you can find the slogan "Good Thinking, Good Products." This slogan was one of the many ideas and innovations that came from employees. Since 1951 when their Creative Idea Suggestion System was introduced, employees have contributed more than 40 million ideas to the company. At one point the implementation rate for these ideas was as high as 98 percent. Not every idea is new and not every idea is worth pursuing but the culture of empowering and enabling employees to innovate is a powerful one. Not only are employees encouraged to come up with ideas but they are also empowered to solve problems when they see them. For example, on the assembly line floor at Toyota plants they have an "Andon" cord, which when pulled, stops the entire assembly line and calls for assistance. When employees see a defect, they pull the cord and fix the problem. One employee at Toyota is empowered to stop an entire assembly line.

Whirlpool, the home appliance manufacturer, is more than 100 years old and has 70,000 employees around the world. A few years ago Whirpool set a goal of moving away from being manufacturing-centric to being innovation-centric. Today, any employee at Whirlpool is encouraged to submit ideas and there is an internal online forum where these ideas are tracked and can be collaboratively developed. There is also a structured process called *idea labs*. Employees come to these sessions with "discoveries" that can be anything from consumer insights to competitive information. These discoveries are not meant to be product ideas, instead they are meant to be insights that can turn into product ideas. Whirlpool is one of the few companies in the world that has made innovation a core competency of everyone's job. Before Whirlpool made this change around innovation its average sales values were declining around 2 percent per year. After it focused on innovation its average sales values have increased 2 percent in aggregate.

Toyota and Whirlpool are just two examples of companies that enable, encourage, and empower employee innovation. 3M, Google, Eli Lilly, Xerox, Tata Group, Best Buy, and many others are all taking a similar approach.

Customer-Driven Innovation

Who better to get advice and ideas from than the people who buy your products and services and interact with your brand? Customers can be a powerful source of innovation.

The coffee giant Starbucks launched a site called "My Starbucks Idea," which has been one of my favorite examples of customer-driven innovation. The site was launched a few years ago but even today is an extremely active site for customer product and service ideas. Customers sign into the platform and can then submit ideas, which are voted on by the community. The team at Starbucks then goes through the ideas to see which ones it can implement. Ideas range from giving free coffees on birthdays to continuing the use of braille on gift cards. Another implemented idea saw Starbucks changing the color of the ink it used to send out its promotional emails. It turns out that the emails had a black background and wasted a lot of ink when customers printed them out. The list of ideas and the customers who contribute are vast and are broken down into product ideas, customer experience ideas, and community involvement ideas. This program has been a core innovation hub for Starbucks and it is completely customer-driven.

FedEx, the global shipping company, needed to find a way to transport live tissues for organ donations. These deliveries needed to always arrive on time with no defects whatsoever. The FedEx team members worked with their customers, who in this case were surgeons, patients, and medical device suppliers, to come up with a solution.

The solution came in the form of a new product called Sensaware, which tracks the package's current location, barometric pressure, temperature, light exposure, and relative humidity, thus giving customers complete insight and visibility into their shipments. This has now been rolled out to international markets and other industries such as aerospace and industrial equipment.

These examples show how powerful and effective customer driven innovation can be.

Partner/Supplier-Driven Innovation

Suppliers are part of the lifeblood for most organizations in the world today. They provide many of the parts, products, or even services that companies then offer to their customers. The simplest example of this can be seen in the retail world when you walk into a store such as Best Buy or Target.

Walmart is one of the world's largest employers with 2.2 million employees, with only the People's Liberation Army of China (2.3 million) and U.S. Department of Defense (3.2 million) having more employees. Walmart understood the importance of supplier innovation decades ago and in the 1980s started sharing its company data, which included things like store level sales and inventory data. At the time Walmart had around $25 billion in annual profit, which was below its main competitors (Sears was at $31 billion and Kmart was at $29 billion). Today Walmart's annual revenue is around $470 billion while Kmart is at $16 billion and Sears is closer to $20 billion. By Walmart sharing its data with suppliers it was able to collaboratively improve forecasting, optimize shelf space, and minimize inventory turnover, which was a win-win for everyone. Recently Walmart developed a program called "Get on the Shelf," which was developed to help small suppliers showcase their products; customers then vote on the products that they want Walmart to sell! Recent innovations include a GPS system for pets, customizable wrist bands, and head covers for chemotherapy patients.

Over the past few years L'Oréal, the cosmetics and beauty company, hosted an event called Cherry Pack[10] where suppliers would come and meet with L'Oréal to discuss everything from new products, packaging, marketing, formulas, and everything else you can think of. They share insights around customer needs and challenges to help make sure that both company and supplier can offer the best and most unique products to customers. Suppliers get feedback so they know what direction they should move toward in terms of product development and L'Oréal gets the products that its customers are looking for. This also helps both parties be more efficient while eliminating waste in terms of time and resources. In the cosmetics and beauty field, the idea of bringing suppliers and company together was rare and unique. In 2012, L'Oréal said it had four major innovations come about as a result of Cherry Pack, one of which is the self-loading pipette for Génifique from Lancôme.

Public-Driven Innovation

Sometimes it can just be the general public that has an idea around a new product or service that can provide mutually beneficial value. It's important for organizations to also be open to ideas from people who are outside of their so-called corporate ecosystem. This can also include education and government contributions as well.

Royal Dutch Shell, the multinational oil and gas company with about 100,000 employees around the world, in 1996 launched a program called GameChanger, which is designed to "nurture unproven ideas that have the potential to drastically impact the future of energy." The program, which was once available only to employees, is now available to anyone on the web. In fact, if you Google "Shell GameChanger" you will find its site where you (and anyone else) can submit an idea. On average, 20 percent of Shell's core R&D program is comprised of ideas or "seeds," which started with GameChanger.

Perhaps the most famous example of an organization opening up its innovation to the world is Procter & Gamble with its Connect &

Develop program. P&G is one of the world's largest consumer products companies in the world with around 130,000 employees. Connect & Develop is a place where P&G puts up all of its "needs," which are essentially problems or challenges that it is trying to tackle. This includes everything from creating products to help repair tooth enamel to pain-free hair removal from the root. Febreze, which is now a more than $1 billion brand, came from Connect & Develop as did the Mr. Clean Magic Eraser and the Crest Spin Brush. In fact, more than 100 new products have been launched as a result of Connect & Develop. Plus, R&D productivity has increased by more than 60 percent and innovation success rates have moved from 15 percent to more than 50 percent. By 2015 P&G wants Connect & Develop to be responsible for more than $3 billion in new business every year.

Many companies are now opening up their innovation process and ideas to anyone. Some of these companies include BMW, LEGO, General Mills, Philips, and Unilever, which has a plethora of challenges ranging from ways to reduce sugar and salt content to finding natural ways to preserve food—again all open for anyone to participate.

Competitor-Driven Innovation

The future organization must realize that sometimes the best talent and ideas can and will come from competitors. Companies must broaden their scope when it comes to innovation. The interesting thing is that this happens informally all the time as colleagues from different organizations get together for casual lunches, meet at conferences, or exchange information on a webinar. Often we hear this referred to as *coopetition*.

Ford and GM, both automotive giants, are perhaps the two fiercest competitors in the world today. However, they decided to work together on developing 9- and 10-speed transmissions to be used in their cars, SUVs, pickup trucks, and crossovers. Both companies realized that they could market faster and cheaper than they could independently. This means they have more collective resources for engineering, testing, design, development, and production. The new product is being developed to go on cars sometime in 2016. The two companies wanted to find a way to develop new gearboxes while improving quality, fuel efficiency, performance, and the standard of technology. Once the transmissions are completed each company will use them on its own cars. Despite being competitors, Ford and GM are teaming up and in doing so will provide mutually beneficial value in the form of a superior, more-advanced product and decreased time to market. Interestingly, Ford is also working with Toyota on developing hybrid powertrains for future pickups.

Recently Boeing and Lockheed Martin teamed up in an attempt to bid on a new U.S. bomber program. Although huge rivals, both companies believe they stand a better chance of winning the multibillion-dollar U.S. Air Force contract from other competitors such as Northrop Grumman. Interestingly, aircraft manufacturer EAD also teamed up with Boeing to develop aviation biofuel to help cut CO emissions.

A few years ago, in response to the rapidly changing technology landscape and growing production demand for TVs, Samsung and Sony teamed up to create something called S-LCD to create new liquid crystal displays (LCD). Each firm invested $1 billion into the project and within a few years they tripled their investment. They also moved up the respective market share leader rankings in LCD TVs, going from third and fourth, respectively, to first and second. In 2011 after a seven-year partnership, Sony sold its stake to Samsung, which now completely owns S-LCD.

The extent of knowledge and innovation used to depend on the organization itself, or more specifically, a few people within the organization. This is no longer enough to maintain a competitive advantage. The future organization must build knowledge ecosystems in the five groups mentioned earlier in order to thrive. Each group can bring a unique perspective and value proposition. For example, employees can bring product and process improvement ideas, customers can come up with relevant marketing and branding ideas, partners and suppliers can improve sales forecasting, the public can be tapped to solve large complex challenges, such as filtering polluted water in third-world countries, and competitors can help with developing superior products and faster time to market.

In an age of constant change and disruption the future organization must think beyond itself in order to succeed and thrive in the future of work.

RUNS IN THE CLOUD

Without getting overly focused on technology it's hard to imagine many organizations not being fully run in the cloud in the next few years. The idea that new technologies need to come from a handful of vendors and have to be installed on-premise is dying. Future organizations will be able to select "best of breed" components from multiple vendors and be able to easily put them together to create systems that work best for them.

Part of the success of the future organization depends on the ability to quickly adapt and technology is part of what allows that to happen. The future organization will not wait 18 months to deal with upgrades or eight months to decide on software purchasing decisions. Virtually every vendor that offers everything from CRM, accounting, collaboration, and HR solutions now has cloud-based products. In fact, to support the future employee the only infrastructure that can be used is the cloud because it's nimble, versatile, and adapts to the flexibility that employees need to work in a distributed world. According to research firm Gartner, global spending on cloud services is expected to reach around $210 billion in 2016.

There are many benefits of running in the cloud. Here are some of the most important ones:

- **Faster deployment time and upgrade time.** Instead of waiting 18 months or more (sometimes two to three years) to deploy or upgrade a piece of software organizations can be up and running or upgraded much faster. For smaller organizations upgrades and deployments happen instantaneously or within a few minutes at most. For larger organizations that have to go through more stringent deployment and upgrade processes this can be as fast as they want it to be, usually a few weeks or a few months. Cloud vendors typically offer upgrades several times a year, which can be rolled out at no cost to the company deploying the technology.

- **Improves flexibility.** Instead of having to rely on a single vendor to provide all your organization's technology requirements, cloud solutions can be used to put together the best features from various vendors. It's a much more customized and flexible approach to technology, which allows organizations to focus on best of breed products.

- **Reduces costs.** In 2013 Rackspace released a report called "88 Per Cent of Cloud Users Point to Cost Savings According to Rackspace Survey"[11] which featured survey results from 1,300 companies in the United States and the United Kingdom. Rackspace found that cloud technologies reduced IT spending 88 percent for cloud users and increased profits for 56 percent of the organizations surveyed. With cloud technologies costs for hardware, storage, maintenance, and security are dramatically reduced or eliminated altogether.

- **Improves accessibility and adoption.** Cloud technologies enable the concept of "anywhere, anytime, and on any device." These technologies allow employees to stay connected to people and information regardless of where they are and in many cases what devices they are using. It's easy for employees to access the people and information they need to get their jobs done. Many cloud technologies are also modeled after popular social applications that we use in our personal lives. In conjunction with the ease of access, cloud technologies are easier to adopt within organizations.

SEES MORE WOMEN IN SENIOR MANAGEMENT ROLES

Today, approximately 16.6 percent of company board seats are occupied by women among the Fortune 1,000 companies. Although the number went up around one percentage point since 2012, it's still not nearly enough. In fact, an organization called 2020 Women on Boards is seeking to get women on 20 percent of company boards by the year 2020. An article published on December 10, 2013 by Catalyst, called "Women in U.S. Management and Labor Force,"[12] showed that in Fortune 500 companies, women only make up 14.6 percent of executive officer positions. Depending on the research, women make up around half of the entire workforce and in some reports women are now the majority of the workforce. Clearly there is gap between women in the workforce and women in leadership roles.

But why women?

The future organization will have more women in senior management roles for several reasons.

Different Perspectives and Points of View

This should come as no surprise. If the future organization relies on a connected workforce to share ideas and uncover opportunities then it also makes sense to have a distributed leadership team comprised of both men and women. In fact, many people believe that if we had more female senior managers during the financial crisis that the whole thing could have been avoided. Sound farfetched? In an article published by the *Daily Mail* on May 8, 2009 called "If Women Had Been in Charge, Would the Economic Crisis Have Happened?"[13] Dr. John Coates, a neuroscientist at Cambridge University who used to work as a trader, was credited with finding evidence that too much testosterone was present on the trading floors. According to the *Daily Mail*, "Dr. John Coates found that when traders had an above-average gain, their testosterone and cortisol levels rose, clouding their judgment and fueling their appetite for risk." Dr. Coates goes on to say, "Women have only 10 percent of the testosterone men have and older men have less than younger men. The trading world is 95 percent young males. If there were more women and older men there might be more stability."

The simple reality is that women have a unique and different perspective on things and we need this diverse and unique perspective to help our organizations come up with new ideas, challenge assumptions, identify opportunities, mitigate risks, and build successful and competitive organizations.

Increased Talent Pool and Access to New Skills

In a March 15, 2012 *Harvard Business Review* article titled "Are Women Better Leaders than Men?"[14] Jack Zenger and Joseph Folkman conducted a survey from almost 7,300 leaders that yielded some interesting results. According to the findings, women are rated higher than men in leadership effectiveness in every single stage of company growth whether they were individual contributors, middle managers, or executives.

The article also went on to reveal that out of the top 16 competencies that leaders exemplify most, women rank higher than men in 15 of them; many by considerable margin. These included things such as: takes initiative, develops others, builds relationships, innovates, technical and professional expertise, collaboration and teamwork, and champions change. In fact, the only area where men narrowly squeaked by was under "develops strategic perspective" where men scored a 51 and women a 49, but in every other area, women rank higher.

Now the aim here isn't to say that women are better than men or vice versa. Instead it is to point out that women are actually very valuable to the future organization and possess many of the desired skills and attributes needed to lead organizations. Men do as well, which is why it's important to have an equal balance.

The management consulting firm McKinsey has a group called McKinsey Women Matter. When this group asked business executives around the world what the most important leadership characteristics are, the top four were: intellectual stimulation, inspiration, participatory decision making, and setting expectations and rewards. According to Women Matter, all four of these qualities were more commonly found among women leaders.

Dr. Alice Eagley, a professor at Northwestern University who specializes in gender differences and leadership styles, writes that there are several unique differences between men and women in leadership. According to Dr. Eagley:

Men's styles are characterized as being:

- Task-oriented
- Autocratic
- Command-and-control
- Punishment-oriented

Women's styles are characterized as being:

- Team players
- Democratic
- Transformational
- Reward-oriented

Clearly this isn't to say that all men lean more toward leadership focused on punishment and all women focus on leadership around rewards. However, this does provide some interesting things to think about and observe in the workforce.

The future organization simply cannot be as competitive without having more women in senior leadership roles.

Accurate Company Representation

If women make up around half of the workforce today and may make up the majority workforce in the future, then why are just a fraction of them in senior leadership roles? Clearly the number of women in the workforce is not reflected by how many of them are in senior positions, which means that many companies around the world are not accurately being represented. This is true when it comes to policies and regulations, best practices, benefits packages, strategic decisions, and anything else that the company needs to do.

The executive teams and corporate boards should be an accurate representation of the company which they help lead. The 2020WOB said it best, "The makeup of corporate boards of directors [and executives] should be representative of the company in which it governs: shareholders, employees, and customers."

Greater Chance of Success

Can it really be true that having more women in senior leadership roles increases the company's chance of succeeding, thriving, growing, and being competitive? Yes!

A 2007 report from Catalyst, called "The Bottom Line: Corporate Performance and Women's Representation on Boards,"[15] found that on average companies with the highest percentage of women on the board of directors achieved a 53 percent higher return on equity than those with the least amount of women on the board of directors. They also achieved 42 percent more return on sales and 66 percent more return on invested capital. Leeds University Business School in London also found that having at least one female director on the board appears to cut a company's chance of going bankrupt by 20 percent. Having two or three female directors lowered the chances of bankruptcy even further.

A white paper called "High Performance Entrepreneurs Women in High Tech,"[16] by Cindy Padnos the founder of Illuminate Ventures, found that women-operated, venture-backed high-tech companies average 12 percent higher annual revenues. She also found that organizations that are the most inclusive of women in top management see a 35 percent higher return on equity and 34 percent better total return to shareholders.

Women Have the Majority Purchasing Power

According to Ginger Consultings' Fifth Annual What Women Want survey released on May 28, 2013,[17] women make up just over 85 percent of all consumer purchasing decisions, including 91 percent of new homes, 66 percent of new PCs, 65 percent of cars, and 80 percent of health-care decisions. Over the next decade women will globally control more than $12 trillion in consumer spending and some estimate this number to be even higher. Their purchasing power is only expected to increase; by 2028 the average American woman is expected to earn more than the average American male. Clearly when it comes to buying things or influencing purchasing decisions women are dominant.

Considering all of this, clearly we should have more women in senior leadership roles because women own the vast majority of purchasing power. We need more women providing their input and ideas on new products and services around the world. Every industry—whether it be technology, real estate, health care, banking, or anything in between—must reconsider and seriously reevaluate the role of women in senior leadership roles. The future organization should understand that because women control and influence the majority of purchasing decisions that it makes sense to have more women in senior leadership roles to represent that market and help capture it. This will be a clear competitive advantage. When taking this into account, it's still a bit shocking that in the United States 36 percent of companies still have no women on their boards of directors.

KPMG is one of the largest professional services firms in the world with over 150,000 employees globally. They are firm believers and more importantly, practitioners, of trying to achieve gender balance in the workplace. Since 2003 the number of female partners at KPMG is up 66 percent. The vice chair of their fastest growing business (advisory) is a woman and so is the national managing partner of their tax practice. In addition, female leaders also run significant offices and other practices across the country. In 2014, more than 41 percent of KPMG's promotions into and within management positions were women and they currently have four women on their board of directors.

Considering the previous statistics in this chapter, I'd say KPMG has done an amazing job of empowering women to have more senior management roles and achieving gender diversity.

It is of course also important to extend this to overall diversity in the workplace which includes other considerations such as race and ethnicity.

FLATTER ORGANIZATIONS AND DECENTRALIZED DECISION MAKING

Most organizations were built on the idea of hierarchy even though the concept was first introduced in the modern business world almost 160 years ago via organizational charts. Chances are that virtually every single person reading this book is familiar with hierarchy in the workplace. A few people at the very top have access to all the relevant business information. They make decisions and then pass their orders and commands down the "food chain." In fact, the very notion that we have to refer to this as a *food chain* should tell us something. Hierarchies are rigid structures that create more boundaries than they help break. Employees don't typically communicate and collaborate across geographies or seniority levels and the structure assumes that organizations are linear, one-dimensional, and that information only flows one way. For the future organization, this type of an approach is detrimental and will prevent a "future" from ever coming to fruition. Hierarchies go completely against what future employees expect and how they will work.

Let's recall a few things. The first is how the future employee is going to work. We know that the future employee is prioritizing things above money and benefits such as workplace flexibility and doing meaningful work. Employees are and will continue to share more information and collaborative technologies are permeating even the most regulated companies around the world. We also know how the role of management is going to change and what the new qualities and characteristics of managers are. Everything mentioned earlier around the future employee and manager goes against why rigid and tall hierarchies exist.

Hierarchies are great for organizations that focus on simple repetitive tasks that don't require any creativity or innovation. In other words, hierarchies are great for drone work where when one cog goes bad it can easily be replaced by another. However, most organizations today depend on creativity, innovation, and employee contributions, which means that strict hierarchies for the most part are inefficient and not effective.

The future organization is going to be much flatter. However, it's safe to assume that most organizations will still retain some form of structure. After all, creating a flat (or flatter) organization doesn't have to mean removing all structure (even though some companies have done that). Many companies such as Google, accounting firm KPMG, Starbucks, Schneider Electric, and others are all trying to "flatten" even though they all still have a somewhat hierarchical structure. In fact, today it's hard to find an organization that says it doesn't want to flatten its structure and I've never met an executive at a company who said, "What we want to do is create more hierarchy, we need more layers."

Flattening an organization, however, isn't just about rearranging an organizational chart, it's about empowering employees to make and participate in decisions and communicate with anyone across the company.

There are several types of emergent organizational structures relevant to the future organization.

Hierarchy

Although the structure shown in Figure 9.2 isn't ideal for the future organization, it's included here for two reasons. The first is so that you can see the comparison with other structures, and the second is because as outdated as this structure is, it's still widely adopted within organizations around the world. This type of environment sees one-way communication from the top down with little collaboration and communication across the organization. It's an outdated way of operating where a few people at the top make the decisions and then delegate down the chain of command. Although this approach used to be the standard, many organizations are now working hard to move toward one of the structures below.

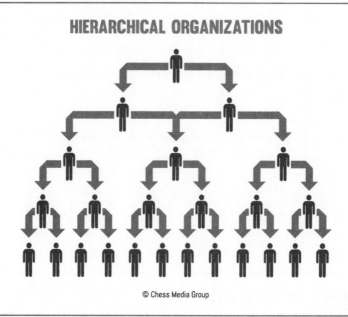

© Chess Media Group

FIGURE 9.2   Hierarchical Organizations

Flatter

The structure in Figure 9.3 is similar to a traditional hierarchy but it's much flatter. How flat it can get depends on what the organization is comfortable with. However, as mentioned earlier creating a flatter organization isn't just about minimizing the chains of command. Flatter companies come about when employees don't need to follow a particular order of communication, decision making, collaboration, and rules, thus minimizing the layers and the barriers between employees at the "bottom" and those at the "top." As you can see in Figure 9.3, communication, connection, and collaboration are open across the whole company. This is the most common approach that many organizations are taking. They are trying to facilitate this by introducing collaboration technologies, which enable this type of open communication, collaboration, and transparency across the company. The reason this approach is the most popular is because it requires the least amount of disruption

FLATTER ORGANIZATIONS

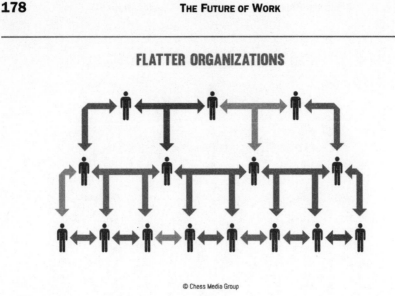

© Chess Media Group

FIGURE 9.3   Flatter Organizations

to the organization. If your organization is looking for a practical and straightforward approach to the future of work then this might be the best alternative.

Flat

Flat organizations (Figure 9.4) are the "valves" of the world, which are completely flat and managerless. As mentioned earlier, informal hierarchies often get created, but from the perspective of an organizational chart there is no power flow, nobody sets the rules and passes them downstream, communication is open, and everyone is on the same footing (ideally). This structure is typically seen in technology companies, start-ups, and some mid-size companies. Employees usually decide the direction of the company and the projects they work on. It's rare to find any large organizations that are completely flat. This approach is relatively popular among smaller organizations or newer ones that are

FLAT ORGANIZATIONS

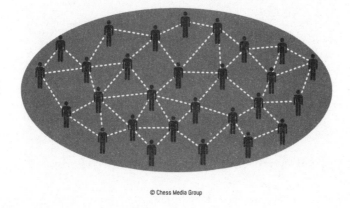

© Chess Media Group

FIGURE 9.4   Flat Organizations

starting off this way. It's hard to imagine any large organization being able to deploy a flat structure. This structure makes the most sense for smaller and newer organizations.

Flatarchies

Flatarchies (Figure 9.5) are organizations that aren't quite flat nor are they hierarchical. They are actually a combination of both types of structures. In other words, an organization can be relatively flat yet can create an ad hoc hierarchy to work on a project or function and then disband. Similarly the organization can have a loose hierarchy that can flatten out when it is required and then return to a loose hierarchy. It's an adaptable model for organizations, which makes it conducive to the freelancer economy. This approach may be the most adaptable but it does require more disruption within the organization to take place. This approach is more relevant to medium- and large-size organizations that are seeking to blend both a solid and loose structure.

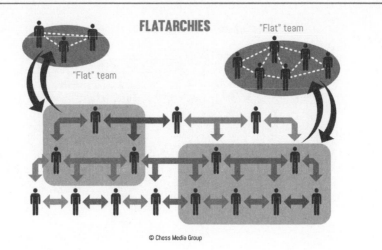

© Chess Media Group

FIGURE 9.5   Flatarchies

Holacratic

This is the approach (Figure 9.6) that organizations such as Zappos and Medium are taking. In fact, Zappos with around 1,500 employees is thus far the largest organization to become holacratic. This approach is based on a circular hierarchy with a strict set of principles for how it should be run and how meetings should be conducted and tensions "processed." Each circle is comprised of several people without any job titles who may have several roles. Circles above others are responsible for setting direction, priorities, and guidance and the circles below are responsible for executing them in an open and democratic way. Holacracy is more common among smaller and some medium-size organizations. At the time of this writing there aren't any larger organizations implementing this approach as it also requires a lot of disruption to the organization to take place.

There is no perfect structure and no perfect approach, and your organization might have other types of structures that it develops.

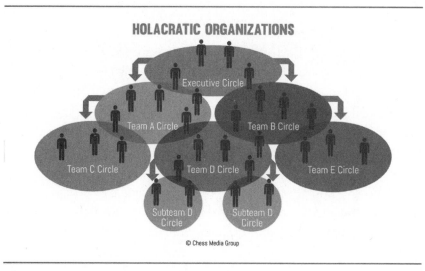

FIGURE 9.6   Holacratic Organizations

Decentralized Decision Making

Often people who see how the world is changing, new opportunities that are emerging, and what needs to be done to adapt, aren't sitting at the top of the organization; yet the ones at the top are the only ones who are empowered to make decisions. This type of an approach isn't scalable, practical, or sustainable for the future organization, especially in a world of rapidly accelerating change. It's simply not possible for a few people to keep steering the ship as the ship keeps growing, new paths are emerging, and more obstacles are forming.

Many years ago I used to work at Whole Foods in Woodland Hills, California as a grocery clerk. I stocked shelves, helped customers, and worked in the dairy cooler and freezer. It still remains one of my favorite jobs. I always had fun showing up to work and loved the people I worked with. I always felt empowered to make decisions without having to get approval for everything and felt that management genuinely cared about the employees and about prosperity. Today, Whole Foods has around 60,000 employees and almost 400 locations.

At Whole Foods each store is empowered to do what is required to meet the needs of its specific customers without always having to get corporate approval. Each store is responsible for its own training, procurement, financials, PR and marketing, and nearly every other critical business decision that needs to be made. Whole Foods' philosophy is to create smaller pieces that are loosely joined together. In effect, when the company grows it actually gets smaller as more decisions get distributed to more people and hierarchy and bureaucracy get reduced. Even at the corporate level decisions are made by a group of several executives who collectively act as a type of CEO council called the E-Team. This team includes John Mackey the Co-CEO, Walter Robb, Co-CEO, A. C. Gallo the president and COO, Glenda Flanagan the EVP and CFO, and Jim Sud the EVP of growth and development.

TELLS STORIES

Why do we like enthralling books, engrossing films, or listening to the many popular TED talks online? Because they all tell powerful stories. Stories allow us to build an emotional connection with a person, brand, product, or company. These stories also help us remember ideas, concepts, and even products. This in turn makes us want to buy from or work for a certain company.

In 1932 in a small town called Billund in Denmark a carpenter by the name of Ole Kirk Christiansen started making high-quality wooden toys. Eventually word of these toys started to spread. After the wholesaler who put in a large order for the toys went bankrupt, Ole drove around to toy stores to sell the toys himself. In Danish the phrase "leg godt" means "play well" and in Latin a similar sounding word means "I put together." LEGO was born. In 1942 the LEGO workshop along with all the toy models and drawings burned to the ground. Ole rebuilt the factory from scratch continuing making high-quality wooden toys. Eventually Ole purchased a plastic molding machine that was first used to create the now famous bricks, which were based on a "system of play." Eventually this allowed children to create LEGO cities, pirate ships, Star Wars models, Harry Potter sets, and even custom sets designed by customers. After near bankruptcy the company is now thriving and today more than 560 billion LEGO parts have been produced. The LEGO story was put together in a video and uploaded on YouTube in 2012 to celebrate their 80th anniversary. Today the video has more than 6 million views.

Customer Stories

Author Simon Sinek has long championed the idea that "people don't buy what you do, they buy why you do it." The "why" can only be addressed by telling a story. Perhaps the best example of company storytelling can be seen with Apple. Starting with Apple's famous "1984" commercial Apple has a long legacy of telling stories. People don't wait in line for hours (or sometimes days) to buy Apple products just because of the new technology. They buy Apple products because it's a form of status. If you buy Apple you are creative, innovative, think outside the box, have an eye for design, and are forward thinking. That's the Apple story, creating beautiful simple products that change your life (and the world). That story has made Apple the most valuable brand in the world today. Apple tells this story in everything it does and in everything it creates.

Employee Stories

At LEGO when a new employee joins the company one of the first things that happens is that they are told the LEGO story—how it started, the challenges that had to be overcome, how it got to where it is today, and where the company can go in the future. In fact, often new employees are taken to the original house and factory that was built by the founder of LEGO, Ole Kirk Christiansen. That factory, which at one point burned to the ground, has now become a powerful symbol for LEGO and a part of its story.

When it comes time to create an organization where employees want to work there instead of need to work there, this idea of storytelling is a powerful resource. Now more than ever employees want to work with organizations that they can relate to, that they can feel proud to work for, and that tell a compelling story. Once your employees can understand and get behind your organization's "why" then they can help you figure out the "how."

DEMOCRATIZE LEARNING AND TEACHING

In most organizations today if you want to learn how to do something you have to take a class offered by a team at your company or with an outside organization. Often this means traveling somewhere, spending the night at a hotel, and having to wait a few days or weeks before you can even take the class. Learning is structured as a linear, process-centric approach, which is a completely outdated way of learning.

If there's anything that the web has taught us it's that learning and teaching don't depend on structure. Anyone with Internet access can go online to find anything they are looking for 24/7 whether it be an article about how to do something, a detailed instructional video on YouTube, or an on-demand class that someone can take from Coursera, Khan Academy, or the many other disruptive educational institutions out there. There is no limit to how much you can learn, how much you can teach, or when and where you can do either.

Thanks to collaborative technologies employees are now able to do the same thing within their organizations. Any employee can learn from anyone else or teach anyone else. This can be done via posting a video from a smart phone or webcam, answering (or asking) a question that someone might have, posting a screenshot or webcast, or anything else. The beauty of using collaborative technologies to do this is that the information is accessible to everyone who might find the information relevant.

The notion of democratized learning is one that enables any employee to become both a teacher and a student thanks to technology.

SHIFT FROM PROFIT TO PROSPERITY

In the Star Trek films and TV series, Spock (played by Leonard Nimoy) didn't say, "Live long and profit," he said, "Live long and prosper."

Profit is quite simply the financial gain that an organization makes. It's the primary measure of success that most organizations in the world use today. Prosperity on the other hand is a word that we don't use as much today. It includes profit but also focuses on things such as health, happiness, and sustainability. Money should not be the only or always primary variable of determining value. Prosperity is a bit more subjective so each organization may have its own version of what it means to be prosperous. However, organizations that focus purely on profits will fail in the long run.

As you see in Figure 9.7 corporations have reached an all-time high in terms of profits. Great right?

Now look at the second graph (Figure 9.8), which looks at the compensation of U.S. employees as a percentage of GDP. You can see that wages are at an all-time low, so companies are making more, but people are making less (as a percentage of the U.S. economy).

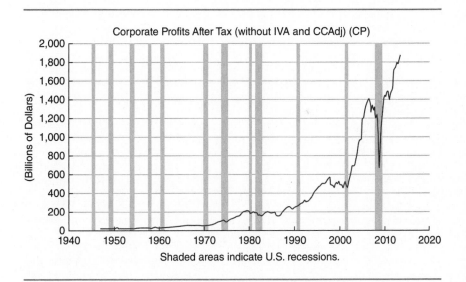

FIGURE 9.7   Corporate Profits After Tax (Without IVA and CCAdj) (CP)

Source: U.S. Department of Commerce: Bureau of Economic Analysis; from 2014 research.stlouisfed.org.

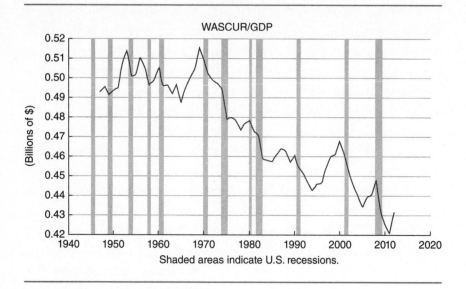

FIGURE 9.8 WASCUR/GDP

Source: 2014 research.stlouisfed.org.

Profits are high but wages are low, 87 percent of workers are sleep-walking through their jobs, and employee retention rates are shrinking. On average, CEOs in the United States make 354 times more than the average worker. To give you some comparison in Japan CEOs make 67 times the amount of the average worker, in Australia 93 times, Germany 147 times, and in the United Kingdom 84 times. These numbers start to get even scarier when you look at specific CEOs; for example, Tim Cook, the current CEO of Apple, makes 6,258 times the amount of the average employee, while Warren Buffett, the CEO of Berkshire Hathaway, makes around 11 times the amount of the average employee. Of course it is true that other factors are also at play here such as the use of automation and robots which are helping improve productivity and profits without the "human" costs associated with doing so.

Edelman released its 2014 Trust Barometer, which surveyed more than 33,000 people around the world. The results showed that only

21 percent of respondents believe that business leaders will make moral and ethical business decisions; this number was only 15 percent for government leaders. When it comes time to telling the truth (regardless of how complex or unpopular it is) again, only 20 percent of respondents believe that business leaders would do so compared to 13 percent of government leaders. These numbers are just as low when it comes to solving social or societal issues as well (19 percent for business leaders and 16 percent for government leaders). Furthermore, the 2013 Trust Barometer study found that treating employees well is the third most important factor when building company trust (61 percent) yet only 24 percent of respondents feel that this is actually happening; this is a massive gap—37 percentage points between importance and performance. These gaps are almost as large in "has ethical business practices" (58 percent importance versus 28 percent performance), "has transparent and open business practices" (57 percent importance versus 24 percent performance), and "takes responsible actions to address an issue or crisis" (58 percent importance versus 25 percent performance). Out of the 16 trust-building attributes, "delivers consistent financial returns to investors" was almost ranked last on the list (tied for second from last).

In their book *Conscious Capitalism: Liberating the Heroic Spirit of Business*, John Mackey and Rajendra Sisodia write, "Business is good because it creates value, it is ethical because it [is] based on voluntary exchange, it is noble because it can elevate our existence, and it [is] heroic because it lifts people out of poverty and creates prosperity."

An advanced degree isn't required to see that something is wrong here. The focus is squarely placed on profits and not on people. It's time for us to ask, "Do high profits make an organization successful?" Unfortunately, Wall Street doesn't share this idea, but it's hard to imagine that things won't change soon. Imagine if entrepreneurs like Steve Jobs, John Mackey, Sergey Brin, and Larry Page or Bill Gates would have had profits as their primary goal when they first started Apple, Whole Foods, Google, or Microsoft. These people didn't know that their companies and inventions would become what they are today. More importantly they didn't start these companies to become millionaires or billionaires, they started them because they loved what they were doing and wanted to change the world. Had profits been their goal from the beginning, chances are none of these companies would exist and instead they would have all taken corporate jobs, which would have paid them a lot more money initially.

The future employee wants to work for an organization that believes and invests in sustainability and community development, corporate social responsibility, health and wellness, employee happiness, ethical choices, and in making the world a better place. In short, the future employee wants to work for an organization that can see beyond itself and one that can contribute to making the world a better place. A 2011 survey by Deloitte, called "The Millennial Survey," found that 92 percent of millennials believe that the success of an organization should be measured by more than just profit. In a recent Bain & Company survey of over 1,200 executives around the world called, "Management Tools & Trends 2013,"[18] 60 percent said they will pursue sustainability initiatives even if it increases their costs. A November 8, 2012 article published by CNN called, "Why Everyone Wants to Work for the 'Good Guys',"[19] cited a study by the Society for Human Resources Management which compared companies with strong sustainability programs versus companies with poor programs. Those with strong programs had 55 percent better morale, 43 percent more efficient businesses processes, 43 percent stronger public image, and 38 percent better employee loyalty. As the title of the CNN article, which references this statistic suggests, everyone wants to work for the good guys. Doing meaningful work is now becoming a top priority, especially among millennials.

The future organizations that are purely driven by profit will always put money ahead of people whereas organizations that are driven by prosperity will put people ahead of money. Profit is no longer the definitive metric of success for an organization even though it might look good on paper.

THE FOUR ROADBLOCKS OF THE FUTURE ORGANIZATION

The world is becoming a faster changing and more turbulent place for organizations and the necessity to adapt has never been greater. To use an analogy, imagine that organizations are boxers stepping into the ring, "change" is the opponent. Larger organizations can be thought of as larger boxers and smaller organizations as smaller boxers. The opponent, "change," starts throwing a few jabs here and there and might land a punch every now and then. Your organization does a good job of blocking them and if you're larger you can easily brush off a few of the hits. As the rounds progress, "change" starts hitting harder and faster. Regardless of how big your organization is or how much money it has, there's only so much it can take before it needs to adapt to the change or risk getting knocked out. So why aren't more organizations (and the people in them) adapting and changing? There are four realistic possibilities for this lack of change: fear of what change means, no urgency to change, uncertainty of how to change, or lack of understanding around what change will bring. Let's take a look at each.

Fear

Any type of change is always met with resistance and the greater the change the more fear we have toward it. We always wonder what will happen if change fails or if things go wrong. It's probably just a safer bet to stay the course. Fear is a powerful motivator to get us to leave things be. However, in this case it's worth exploring what there is to be fearful of. The future organization is simply adapting to the changes that are already taking place. It's not about investing in a new billion-dollar prototype, moving into a new market segment, or debating on whether to open an international office. It's about adapting to changes in behavior. Thought of in this context it's worth reframing the question from "Should we be scared to change?" to "We should be scared not to change!"

No Urgency

It's understandable, your organization has a list of priorities and the future of work is not anywhere near the top of that list. That's fine. But consider that every single one of your existing priorities, whether it be investing in new technologies, corporate restructuring, an acquisition, or anything else, are all impacted by the future of work. How employees work and how managers lead impacts every single facet of your organization, which is why the future of work should be at the very top of your organization's priority list and not at the bottom.

Uncertainty

Many organizations understand that the world of work is changing, they just don't know what to do about it. They don't understand why the changes are happening or what the change is going to look like. Hopefully this book took care of that by providing a picture of what the future of work looks like for employees, managers, and organizations as a whole. Use these several hundred pages as a way to progress towards change at your organization.

Unclear Impact

What will change bring? This is a common question and a fair one to ask. In this case change isn't an endpoint as much as it is the ability to continuously adapt. The impact from this is creating an organization where employees want to work, where managers lead effective teams, and where organizations shift from becoming profitable to becoming prosperous. In short, the impact is creating an organization that survives and thrives and perhaps becomes immortal.

THE EVOLUTION OF THE ORGANIZATION

To better understand all of the changes that organizations are having to adapt to, take a look at Figure 9.9.

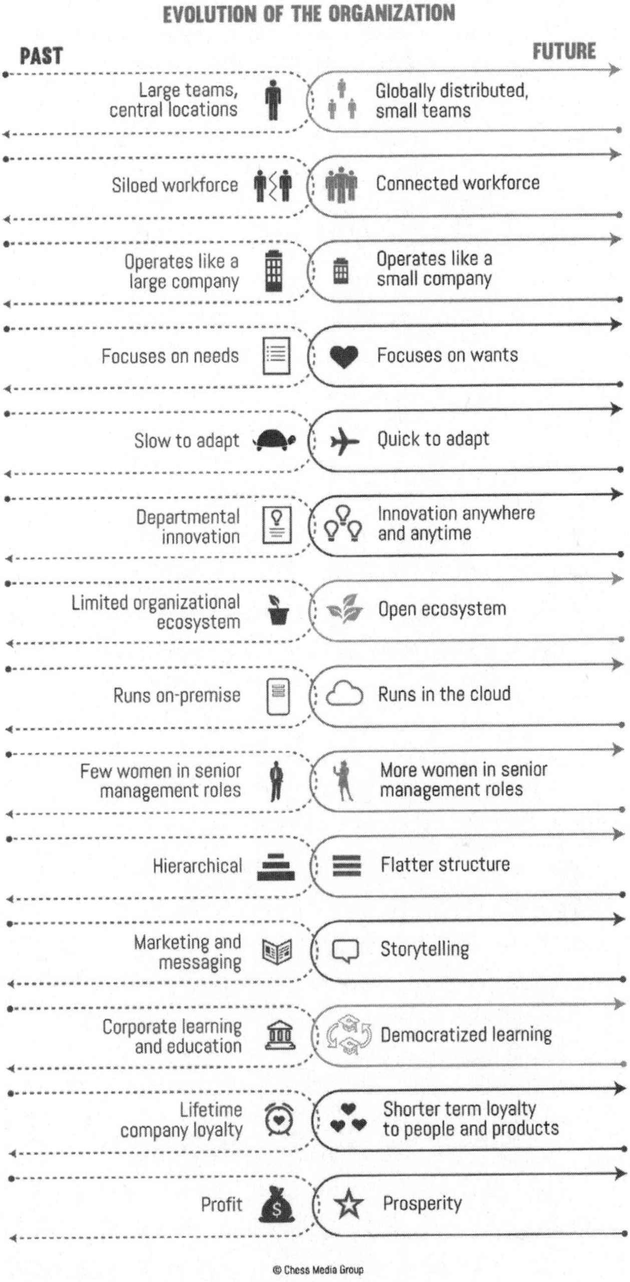

EVOLUTION OF THE ORGANIZATION

PAST   FUTURE

Large teams,   Globally distributed,
central locations   small teams

Siloed workforce   Connected workforce

Operates like a   Operates like a
large company   small company

Focuses on needs   Focuses on wants

Slow to adapt   Quick to adapt

Departmental   Innovation anywhere
innovation   and anytime

Limited organizational   Open ecosystem
ecosystem

Runs on-premise   Runs in the cloud

Few women in senior   More women in senior
management roles   management roles

Hierarchical   Flatter structure

Marketing and   Storytelling
messaging

Corporate learning   Democratized learning
and education

Lifetime   Shorter term loyalty
company loyalty   to people and products

Profit   Prosperity

© Chess Media Group

FIGURE 9.9   Evolution of the Organization

CHAPTER 10

Technology as the Central Nervous System

As mentioned earlier, technology is the central nervous system or the backbone of the future organization. However, technology is a broad term that can refer to almost anything. The core types of technologies that are really enabling the future organization are all centered on collaboration; in other words, getting people to share and work together. These technologies include everything from web-conferencing tools and task management applications to full internal social networks deployed within organizations.

Most organizations today have either deployed various collaboration technologies or are in the process of doing so. Unfortunately, the big challenge around these new technologies is actually getting employees to use them. After all, if employees don't use the technologies then things like flexible work, customized work, real-time recognition, collective intelligence, and many of the other things mentioned in this book are not possible. Simply said, there is no future organization without technology, and, specifically, collaboration technology.

Although a detailed strategic framework around collaboration was covered in my previous book, *The Collaborative Organization*, what wasn't addressed were the lowest common denominators that make organizations successful. In other words, what are some of the common things that the successful organizations are doing to help with adoption of collaborative technologies?

THE 12 HABITS OF HIGHLY COLLABORATIVE ORGANIZATIONS

Chess is a virtually limitless game, yet we still have grandmasters who spend lots of time studying games and pondering moves. What for? Why bother trying to study or explore something if the combinations are endless: to identify patterns and look for familiar scenarios or positions. This approach also makes sense when it comes to technology adoption. Every organization will have different business drivers, budgets, responsible departments, technologies that are selected, and many other things. In short, no two companies are alike. However, in researching and speaking with many companies over the past few years I was able to identify 12 habits that the successful organizations are doing to get their employees to use collaboration technologies:

1. Focus on individual value before corporate value.
2. Strategy always comes before technology.
3. Learn to get out of the way.
4. Lead by example.
5. Listen to the voice of the employee.
6. Integrate into the flow of work.
7. Create a supportive environment.
8. Measure what matters.
9. Be persistent.
10. Adapt and evolve.
11. Understand that employee collaboration also benefits the customer.
12. Accept that collaboration makes the world a better place.

Let's look at these 12 habits in a bit more detail to see what they actually represent in the workplace.

Individual Value before Corporate Value

When the majority of companies deploy collaborative technologies (or any technology for that matter) they tend to always focus on the corporate value that can be derived as a result. They may say something like, "We are very excited to roll out our new collaboration platform to help us improve productivity, identify new business opportunities, and help us figure out where we can reduce costs." All valuable things to the company and all valueless things to the employees. If employees are going to be using the technologies then they need to understand the value that these technologies can bring to them as individuals. Will this new collaboration platform make it easier for them to find people and information at work? Will the amount of content duplication be reduced? Will employees have a better understanding of how their contributions are impacting the team? Will they now be able to have a more flexible work environment? These are the things that matter to employees. Focus on them.

Strategy before Technology

Common sense right? Unfortunately as the saying goes, "Common sense is not that common." It's constantly surprising how many organizations deploy technologies without knowing why they are doing so to begin with, and these technologies are not cheap! To give you an analogy this is like walking into a hardware store, buying a million-dollar (or more) hammer, and then taking it home to try to fix all of your structural problems. This is a common, costly, and time-consuming trap that many organizations fall into only to later realize that the technology they deployed wasn't really ideal for what they needed.

Before buying that hammer why not do a walk-through of your metaphorical house to see where the problems are and then figure out the best tools you need to use to solve those problems. Understanding the "why" before you understand the "how" is a relatively simple yet crucial thing that successful organizations do.

Learn to Get Out of the Way

Pretend I'm the CEO of your company and tomorrow at our "all-hands" meeting I walk into the conference room and say, "Starting tomorrow you can wear anything you want to work as long as it's with a suit and tie." You would probably be a bit confused and think I'm off my rocker. Yet this is the exact message that many organizations send to their employees who are trying to deploy collaboration technologies. Organizations may say, "You can use the tools but don't mentioned our brands by name," "You can join groups but you can't create them," "Share information but only if it's work-related," "Use the collaboration tools but only on the devices we approve," "Create your own profile but we have to approve it." The list goes on and on. Basically organizations are telling employees, "We want you to be collaborative and empowered but it has to be our way," which defeats the whole point of these technologies. Organizations can provide guidelines, best practices, and helpful tips but they must learn to get out of the way by giving employees as much freedom as they can get away with.

Lead by Example

This is one of the principles for the future manager, but it's also extremely applicable to the world of technology. An unfortunate mistake that organizations make is assuming that managers don't need to use the same technologies that everyone else is using. If managers aren't using collaboration technologies then why should employees bother using them? The concept of leading by example relies on the fact that using collaboration technologies isn't a mandate given to employees. The best way to get employees to use new technologies is to lead by example.

Listen to the Voice of the Employee

We've all heard the popular mantra, "Listen the voice of the customer," but what about the voice of the employee? Organizations spend a lot of time and resources looking outward and often forget to look inward at the very people who are servicing the customers, steering the ship, creating the strategies, and building the products. Thanks to collaboration technologies employees now have a voice where they can share feedback, ideas, passions, and anything else. This means that organizations need to pay attention to and listen to the things that employees have to say and make changes when relevant.

Integrate into the Flow of Work

Chances are that you and all the other employees at your organization are already busy at work. You are working on multiple projects, attend various meetings, travel to meet with clients, and already use many technologies to help make your work possible. You don't really have the time to throw yet another piece of technology into the mix. It's just another username and password and yet another place you need to log into to get your job done. This is why it's so important for collaboration platforms to not be stand-alone or additional technologies that employees have to use. Think of these technologies as collaborative operating systems where you go to get all of your work done and from where you can access anything and everything else you need—they are the "front door" to your organization.

Create a Supportive Environment

Technology is and always will be an enabler; it allows people to do things, but if they don't use the technology then it's pointless. This means that creating an environment that encourages collaboration in the workplace is essential. If you think of an organization that says it wants to be open and collaborative and one that encourages sharing, you typically don't think of an organization comprised of endless rows of cubicles where everyone comes to work wearing formal attire. Yet for some reason that's exactly what's happening in organizations. I call this the *online dating effect*. In other words, organizations are publicly portraying themselves as being a certain way but the reality is that they are completely opposite. You can't be collaborative and open in an environment where everyone sits in a cubicle, where stack ranking is the primary method of performance review, and where employees are rewarded based solely on financial performance.

Creating a supportive environment means taking actions that help support the desired behaviors that you want your employees to exhibit. The physical and real-world environment needs to emulate the virtual one you are seeking to create via collaboration platforms. Examples of creating a supporting environment can include everything from changing the physical space of where employees work (such as removing cubicles), to education and training opportunities on collaboration (such as Friday lunch and learns or weekly virtual discussions), to changing core parts of how the organization operates (such as removing stack rankings, changing how employees are hired and incentivized).

Measure What Matters

Collaboration technologies can yield all sorts of statistics such as the number of employees who might be using the platform, number of discussions, number of groups, visits, most active contributors, and dozens of other things. Although it's nice to have an understanding of what all of these metrics are and what they mean, it's important to not focus on everything under the sun. The key metrics to look at are the ones that matter—in other words, the metrics that are going to help you understand if you are meeting the objectives you set out to meet. If your focus is on innovation then you will be looking at things such as new ideas that employees have submitted, how many of those ideas turned into products, how long it takes to turn an idea into a product, and how much revenue those employee-driven products are generating.

The important thing is that data can come in many ways, whether it is numbers or unstructured employee survey data such as asking your employees if they feel that they are being more productive. Whatever it is you choose to measure make sure it goes back to the business case you have set up. Measure smart and measure regularly.

Be Persistent

You probably don't remember when you first started walking, but I can guarantee that when you first got up on your two feet and stumbled your parents didn't look at each other and say, "Maybe walking isn't for our baby." Chances are that every time you fell you were met by words of support and encouragement, urging you to get back up and try again. We have all been faced with challenges in our lives and if we were to give up at the first sign of an obstacle, we wouldn't have gotten very far in life.

Let me be the first to tell you that you will run into obstacles and challenges: everything from budgetary issues, managers who don't support your cause, IT teams that won't budget security issues, employees who refuse to use the technologies, and a host of other things. That's fine, just know that these things will come up and then you will have to work your way through them and keep moving forward.

Adapt and Evolve

I've always been a fan of kung-fu movies and one of my favorite martial artists has always been the great Bruce Lee. Bruce Lee has a fantastic quote that speaks to adaptability, "You must be shapeless, formless, like water. When you pour water in a cup, it becomes the cup. When you pour water in a bottle, it becomes the bottle. When you pour water in a teapot, it becomes the teapot. Water can drip and it can crash. Become like water my friend."

There is no endpoint for the future of work or collaboration. New technologies, behaviors, and approaches to work are always going to be on the horizon. Adapting and evolving means paying attention to trends and being able to implement the necessary changes at your organization to keep up.

Understand That Employee Collaboration Also Benefits the Customer

Many organizations forget that employee collaboration and engagement also benefits the customer. If a customer has a question or an issue that they need resolved your employees can provide a faster, more accurate, and more in-depth response by tapping into the collective knowledge base of the organization. Not only that but a valuable knowledge repository can be created to help customers answer their own questions in the future.

Collaboration also benefits employees by making their overall work experience better. As mentioned earlier in this book, the employee experience tends to emulate the customer experience, which means that if your employees have a positive experience your customers are more likely to have a positive experience as well.

Accept That Collaboration Makes the World a Better Place

Creating an organization that embraces collaborative approaches and technologies has dramatic benefit for employees inside and outside of the workplace. At work employees will be able to leverage flexible work environments, reduce content duplication, find people and information easier, be more engaged, and get a greater sense of alignment and fulfillment.

Outside of work this means that employees will be less stressed and will have more time to spend with their families. They will have fewer arguments with their spouses and will feel less stress. They will see an overall improvement in quality of life, well-being, and happiness. For the first time, organizations are able to invest in something that not only positively impacts the lives of employees at work but also outside of work.

It might sound idealistic but many of the employees I have spoken with whose organizations are making these investments are noticing these benefits in their lives and that's a powerful thing.

These are the 12 habits that the successful organizations are practicing to make their collaboration initiatives thrive. I highly recommend you implement these within your organization as well!

CHAPTER 11

The Six-Step Process for Adapting to the Future of Work

How to Become the Future Organization (and Stay That Way!)

Successfully creating a future organization that can adapt to the future employee and the future manager requires a new and fresh approach to facilitating change. Essentially the goal is to create a process whereby the organization is able to adapt to the future of work regardless of how many years out that future might be. You can expect constant gradual change with major change happening every few years. Dr. John Kotter pioneered a change management model called the "8-Step Process for Leading Change," which inspired me to create a model of my own specifically focused on the future of work. Based on researching and speaking with many organizations (some of which are mentioned in this book), the model looks like Figure 11.1.

1. Challenge assumptions.
2. Create a team to help lead the effort.
3. Define your "future of work."
4. Communicate your "future of work."
5. Experiment and empower employees to take action.
6. Implement broad-based change.

THE 6 STEP PROCESS FOR ADAPTING TO THE FUTURE OF WORK

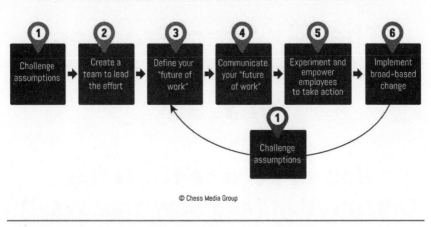

© Chess Media Group

FIGURE 11.1 **The Six-Step Process for Adapting to the Future of Work**

CHALLENGE ASSUMPTIONS

The first step for any organization to become a future organization is to challenge and question the conventional practices and ways of doing things within the organization. The sections in this book give you plenty of fodder to get you started. Too often we take things at face value without really understanding why things are done the way they are or if there are better ways of doing something. Anyone within your organization has the opportunity to challenge or question something or to explore alternate ways of getting something done. This isn't just reserved for managers.

There are two components to this.

Ask

Why aren't employees allowed to make decisions? Why don't we have collaborative technologies at work? Why are employees commuting two hours every day to get to work? You cannot challenge and question conventional practices without asking something. Figure out the questions you want to ask. Simple enough right? This can be done via in-person discussions, meetings, one-on-ones, surveys, or any other way you are comfortable with. Instead of focusing on specific tactical questions focus on broader policies or approaches that have a broader and overarching impact on the organizations. Most of the employees will be able to relate to these things. In progressive organizations these challenges are done in a public way, not behind closed doors. The more people can see the challenges the better.

Listen

In a typical conversation when you ask someone something you get an answer. In this case the questions you ask will be answered by employees, managers, and other stakeholders. The challenging step of this process doesn't work if you don't listen to the responses that you get back. Pay specific attention to how things are justified or explained. Often you will find areas with no rational explanation other than, "That's how it has always been." The listening approach will help you clearly identify where your quick wins will be and where you will face the greatest challenges.

CREATE A TEAM

Organizations such as Whirlpool and Xerox have teams devoted to understanding and studying how the world of work is changing and how those changes are going to impact their organizations. These teams not only conduct research, they put in place new programs to actually help make changes happen including training and education. This is enormously helpful for organizations as it makes the future of work a real and tangible part of the organization that other employees can turn to for guidance and direction. As the rate of change continues to increase it's important to know that you have a dedicated team at your company that is keeping pace.

The future of work has no endpoint. Several years after this book is published it will be time to write another one that explores a different future. The team you create should be a dedicated team focused on helping your organization understand what the future of work will look like and what steps need to be taken to adapt to that future. This team will be responsible for:

- Defining what the future of work looks like.
- Educating and training employees.
- Researching trends both internally and externally.
- Developing strategies and approaches.
- Experimenting.
- Communicating the future of work to the organization.
- Empowering employees to make change.
- Implementing broad-based change programs.

The team that will shape the future of work at your organization is crucial for success. This is the engine that will keep everything going. The team structure can vary quite a bit in each organization but there are a few important qualities to pay attention to:

- **Recognized leadership:** Executive sponsors and recognized leaders within the organization are important for credibility and visibility.
- **Resources:** The team must have the people and financial resources in place to research, test, and implement ideas.
- **Power to experiment:** Being able to test out ideas is crucial. Not every idea or concept will make sense but there needs to be a way to figure out what works and avoid what doesn't.
- **Ear of executives:** There should be a direct line of communication with the executive team, especially because the team itself will include at least one executive sponsor.

- **Known to the company:** The team's existence and their mission must be communicated to the company. Employees should know that this team exists, what they are working on, and who is a part of the team. Contacting them should be easy.

DEFINE

The majority of this book is focused on helping you understand what the future of work will look like. But every organization will have differences, things it wants to focus on, and essentially its own vision and goal for what its future of work will look like. You can easily follow the principles in this book and stick to them or you can use them as a starting point and adapt, edit, and change them. But what the future of work looks like at your organization will depend on how you define a few things that are quite common but rarely thought about:

Work: What does it mean to work at your company? Is it a simple exchange where people come in, do a job, get paid, and then leave? Is "work" at your company drudgery? How do employees work? How has your understanding and definition of work changed?

Employee: What does an employee look like at your company? Is everyone a type of leader? Do employees serve managers? Why do employees work at your organization? What does the future employee look like and how is he or she different from the employee of the past?

Manager: What makes a manager at your company? Is it someone who brings in money or someone who engages people? What is the role and the function of the manager? How is the manager of the future different from the manager of the past?

Organization: What does it mean to work at your organization and what does it value? Is your organization changing the way it operates or the way it's structured? How does the organization of the past compare to the organization of the future that you want to create?

COMMUNICATE

There's no point coming up with a vision for the future of work if nobody in your organization knows what that vision is or what to do about it. In this case "communicate" means more than holding a town-hall meeting, sending out an email newsletter, or writing a blog post about it. The successful organizations follow a few guidelines to help make sure their vision for the future of work gets seen and heard, loud and clear.

Make It Public

Getting the word out to employees is great but when you publicly tell the world what kind of organization you want to become and what the future of work looks like, then it becomes something that employees can stand behind. Unilever does an excellent job of this by clearly communicating its concept of agile working and sustainable living for the world to see. This is complete with employee and executive video interviews, which are found on the Unilever "careers" page. Unilever is now synonymous with agile working. Anytime people think of working at your organization they should immediately know about your vision for the future of work. Share it in presentations, press releases, meetings, and any time an employee makes a public presentation about your company.

Make It Easy and Relatable

If someone were to ask you, "What is it like working at your company?" or "What's the future of work at your company?" what would you tell them? Whirlpool would probably tell you that it wants to create a winning workplace where every employee is an empowered leader who can solve customer problems. If you recall from earlier in the book, Whirlpool has a clear set of foundational principles that comprise its Winning Workplace. You don't need to come up with something overly complex, jargon-filled, or long: something simple like, "creating an adaptable and engaged organization where every employee is empowered to solve problems and come forward with ideas." You get the idea.

Break It Down

Having the big picture vision is a great starting point but often people want to know what that means and what changes are going to come as a result. So if we were to use the Whirlpool example earlier, you might say, "How do we create an adaptable and engaged organization where employees are empowered to solve customer problems and come forward with ideas?" Well, this might entail things such as deploying collaborative technologies, creating an open communication policy, hosting idea jam sessions, enabling flexible work environments, and a host of other things. These action items are important to break down so that employees get a sense of what changes to expect and why those changes are happening.

EXPERIMENT AND EMPOWER

Change is the only constant and in that type of an environment the only way to know what works and what doesn't is by trying things out. Every experiment is a chance to learn what works and what doesn't.

After conveying what the future of work at your organization can become and what some of the changes might look like, you then want to give employees the ability to help create change. At this stage the changes are most likely going to be departmental or team-based, but they are still crucial to have. Keep in mind the goal of the team leading this initiative is to experiment so this is where that comes into play. Test things out to see what works in various parts of the organization before making broad-based change (which is the next step). However, if your team or department is able to make change happen without broader corporate involvement, then go for it! Change always happens gradually, which means more experiments more often.

In order to empower employees a few things must be considered.

Identify Areas with Large Gaps

In most organizations there are typically some more forward-thinking and progressive teams and those that appear to be still working with sticks and stones. These are the teams that require the most urgent support as their employees are often the most disengaged. Identifying the teams with the largest gaps can easily be done by having conversations with team members or by conducting quarterly employee surveys. Once these are identified then incremental changes can be made.

Remove Obstacles

We are talking about smaller changes to groups or departments, so chances are that each segment will have its own obstacles that need to be overcome. In some areas this might be managers who just refuse to change, in others it might be policies that have been followed for years that were never questioned, technology limitations are another possibility, and so could an overly competitive environment where employees don't feel comfortable working in a team setting. So for your particular area, team, department, or geography you want to make sure you understand what these obstacles are and then come up with solutions to remove them. You might deploy collaboration technologies, train managers, or remove an outdated incentive program.

Give Permission

Once the obstacles are removed (or corrected) employees need to actually be allowed to change behaviors. This might mean letting them try out flexible work, not having to ask for permission for every purchase they might want to make, or giving them visibility into information typically reserved just for managers. Let employees exhibit the behaviors and actions that support your vision and definition for the future of work.

Not everything will work out the way you think it will or the way you might want it to and that's fine. The point of experimenting and empowering is to be able to replicate successes while removing things that are not effective. The more experiments you can make, the more often you can make them better. You don't need to have yearlong drawn-out pilot programs either, try to keep things moving as fast as possible.

IMPLEMENT BROAD-BASED CHANGE

This is the type of change that can be made across the entire organization. For example, your organization might implement a sweeping flexible work policy across the company. Talent management strategies might be revisited to remove annual reviews and instead replace them with more frequent and less lengthy employee check-ins. Promotions may focus on rewarding the best collaborators instead of those who bring in the most money. Employees can shed their "manager" titles to help remove hierarchy within the organization. Stack-ranking may be replaced by a more collaborative approach. Whatever the changes are that your organization seeks to implement, this is where that gets done. You should have plenty of learnings from your experiments that you can apply. A few things to consider.

Plan

Change obviously doesn't happen overnight, it does require some planning. Ask yourself the following questions when planning:

- When do we want specified changes to take place?
- What are the easiest and most valuable things that can be changed?
- What is the ongoing roadmap for any subsequent changes?
- How will we encourage change among employees and managers?
- If something isn't received well by employees are we going to revert to the way things were?

It's tempting to spend a long time trying to craft the perfect strategy or the perfect plan, but there is no such thing. The best way to learn to swim is by jumping in the pool. You will learn as you go once you have some of the basic questions answered.

COMMIT

One of the biggest mistakes that organizations make when it comes to the future of work is saying that it wants to commit to doing something and then not doing anything about it, or doing something for a short period of time. If there is no commitment then there will be no success. The principles described in this book are not a fad or a trend, they are not going to disappear and things will not revert to the way they were decades ago. Your organization must make a conscientious and purposeful choice to adapt to the way employees work, the way managers lead, and the way your institution operates.

Organizations that follow this approach will help ensure that it continuously adapts to the changes happening in the world of work.

CHAPTER **12**

Rethinking Work

There are always people who believe that they don't need to change; companies that believe they are too big to fail. If things are going fine as is, than why bother doing anything differently? Many companies innovate and change when they have to. In other words, they wait for something bad to happen for their company to "dip" and then they focus on innovation to bring them back to the status quo; sadly this puts the company in the same position it was just before tragedy struck; that's not adaptation, that's keeping your head above water. The successful organizations change and challenge when things are going well so that they can rise above the status quo, so while others are keeping their heads above water, they are growing and innovating. To put it simply, if you don't think about and plan for the future of work then your company has no future.

If you read this book and come away thinking that you can wait or that the themes and topics in this book are not a priority then unfortunately I didn't do a good enough job in helping to paint a picture of the future of work. But I hope that's not the case. I sincerely hope that every reader will at least walk away from this book understanding change is happening and it's time to rethink work.

The next few years are going to be very exciting and full of opportunities for employees, managers, and organizations as a whole. We are seeing remarkable changes that are impacting the way we work, the way we lead and manage, the way organizations are run, and the way in which we think about work in general. The future of work doesn't see the employee as a cog, a manager as a slave-driver, the organization as a gang, and work as drudgery. Instead, all of these roles and components of work will be thought of as something more.

Work is an experience that is designed by both the organization and by all of the employees who are participating in it. The created experience not only benefits the organization but also the person(s) doing the activity. The employee doing the work receives value beyond just a paycheck and although subjective it can include personal satisfaction, empowerment, happiness, a sense of fulfillment and accomplishment and other nonfinancial benefits. Work is not drudgery, it's an opportunity for employees to embark on a journey with an organization (or several) that they believe in and care about and one that reflects their values.

Employees are people who work at organizations because they *want* to not just because they *need* to. They believe in what the company does, enjoy their job, the people they work with, and the company they are a part of. Employees shape their career paths, have a voice, and will be engaged at work. They genuinely enjoy the work that they do. Employees work anywhere, anytime, and on any device. They are global, diverse, and connected. In a few years when I keynote a conference and ask people what makes them happy, "work" will be a common answer.

Managers are leaders who believe in serving employees and empowering them, not controlling them or micro-managing them. Managers believe that employees are valuable assets to the organization, not cogs. They value their feedback, ideas, and suggestions and want and enable them to succeed by removing obstacles from their path. Managers believe in flexible work environments and want employees to be happy and accountable for the work they do. Managers challenge common ideas around leadership, they are fire starters, and they help work get done.

Organizations are institutions that design employee (and customer) experiences and believe in and foster employee engagement. They believe in breaking down boundaries, giving employees a voice, and focusing on the quality of work that gets done instead of where it gets done. Organizations believe in workplace flexibility and in creating a place where employees want to work, not where they need to work. They adapt to change faster and are flatter and less hierarchical in nature; a few of them don't even have managers. Organizations are places where the future employee and the future manager thrive.

How you define these things for your organization is going to make all the difference. What kind of an environment do you want to work in and what kind of a company do you want to work with? There has never been a greater opportunity for employees, managers, organizations, and for you to take advantage of the changes we are seeing in the world of work. But this can't be done without challenging convention.

Remember, if you don't think about and plan for the future of work, then your organization will have no future!

Notes

CHAPTER 1 THE FIVE TRENDS SHAPING THE WORLD OF WORK

1. John Gantz and David Reinsel, "Extracting Value from Chaos," *IDC Report* (June 2011).
2. Phone interview with Hans Haringa about GameChanger program.
3. Phone interview conducted with Mark Howorth.
4. "Gartner Says the Internet of Things Installed Base Will Grow to 26 Billion Units by 2020," press release, December 12, 2013, www.gartner.com/newsroom/id/2636073.
5. Aaron Smith, "Smartphone Ownership 2013," Pew Research Internet Project, June 5, 2013.
6. John Heggestuen, "One in Every 5 People in the World Own a Smartphone, One in Every 17 Own a Tablet," *Business Insider* (December 15, 2013).
7. Andrew McAfee and Erik Brynjolfsson, "Investing in the IT That Makes a Competitive Difference," *Harvard Business* (July 2008).
8. Phone interview with Dr. John Kotter.

CHAPTER 2 THE COG: TODAY'S EMPLOYEE

1. Gallup, "The State of the Global Workplace: Employee Engagement Insights for Business Leaders Worldwide," 2013. PDF available for download at www.gallup.com/strategicconsulting/164735/state-global-workplace.aspx.
2. "Employee Engagement and Retention," Kelly Global Workforce Index (2013).
3. Y. Hong, H. Liao, J. Hu, and K. Jiang, "Missing Link in the Service Profit Chain: A Meta-Analytic Review of the Antecedents, Consequences, and Moderators of Service Climate," *Journal of Applied Psychology* 98, no. 2 (March 2013): 237–267.
4. Anahad O'Connor, "The Claim: Heart Attacks Are More Common on Mondays," the *New York Times*, March 14, 2006.
5. PricewaterhouseCoopers, "State of the Workforce: PwC Saratoga's 2013/ 2014 US Human Capital Effectiveness Report," July 2013, www.pwc.com/us/en/hr-management/publications/human-capital-effectiveness-state-of-workforce-report .jhtml.

CHAPTER 3 SEVEN PRINCIPLES OF THE FUTURE EMPLOYEE

1. Jessica Krinkle, "The Age of Agility," *Talent Management* (May 2, 2012) http://talentmgt.com/articles/view/the-age-of-agility.
2. Chess Media Group, "The Future of Work: Reshaping the Workplace Today. Building for Tomorrow," 2013, www.chessmediagroup.com/resources/research-reports/the-future-of-work-research-report.
3. Joshua Bjerke, "Employees Prefer Flexibility over Salary Increases," Recruiter.com (August 31, 2012).
4. U.S. Census Bureau, "Megacommuters: 600,000 in U.S. Travel 90 Minutes and 50 Miles to Work, and 10.8 Million Travel an Hour Each Way, Census Bureau Reports," March 5, 2013, https://www.census.gov/newsroom/releases/archives/american_community_survey_acs/cb13-41.html.
5. Society for Human Resource Management, "SHRM Poll: Challenges Facing Organizations and HR in the Next 10 Years," September 16, 2010.
6. "Long Commutes 'Bad for Marriage': Swedish Study," May 24, 2011, www.thelocal.se/20110524/33966.
7. Jim Harter and Nikki Blacksmith, "Engaged Workers Immune to Stress from Long Commutes," Gallup (February 7, 2012), www.gallup.com/poll/152501/engaged-workers-immune-stress-long-commutes.aspx.
8. Global Workplace Analytics, www.globalworkplaceanalytics.com/telecommuting-statistics.
9. Kathy Gurchiek, "Can a Mobile Workforce Better Serve Citizenry?" Society for Human Resource Management, September 17, 2013, www.shrm.org/hrdisciplines/technology/Articles/Pages/Can-a-Mobile-Workforce-Better-Serve-Citizenry.aspx.
10. Phone interview with Schneider Electric.
11. Adam Vaccaro, "Number of Coworking Spaces Has Skyrocketed in the U.S.," *Inc.* (March 3, 2014), www.inc.com/adam-vaccaro/coworking-space-growth.html.
12. Phone interview with Treehouse; information was also taken from this series published by the CEO (Ryan Carson), "No Managers: Why We Removed Bosses at Treehouse," http://ryancarson.com/post/61562761297/no-managers-why-we-removed-bosses-at-treehouse.
13. Cathy Benko and Anne Weisberg, "Mass Career Customization: Building the Corporate Lattice Organization," Deloitte University Press, August 1, 2008.
14. The Valve Employee Handbook can be found here, scroll down: www.valvesoftware.com/jobs/index.html.
15. Joshua Brustein, "Microsoft Kills Its Hated Stack Rankings. Does Anyone Do Employee Reviews Right?" *Businessweek* (November 13, 2013).
16. "Email Statistics Report, 2013–2017," The Radicati Group, April 22, 2013.
17. "The Shape of Email," Mimecast, October 2012.
18. "Email Statistics Report, 2011–2015," The Radicati Group (May, 2011).

19. Shamsi T. Iqbal and Eric Horvitz, "Disruption and Recovery of Computing Tasks: Field Study, Analysis, and Directions," Proceedings of the SIGCHI Conference on Human Factors in Computing Systems (2007), 677–686.

20. Thomas L. Friedman, "Need a Job? Invent It," the *New York Times*, March 30, 2013.

21. Blake Ellis, "Class of 2013 Grads Average $35,200 in Total Debt," *CNNMoney*, May 17, 2013.

22. Richard Vedder, Christopher Denhart, and Jonathan Robe, "Why Are Recent College Graduates Underemployed? University Enrollments and Labor-Market Realities," Center for College Affordability and Productivity, January 2013.

23. Richard Vedder, "End U.S. Student Loans, Don't Make Them Cheaper," Bloomberg (July 17, 2012).

24. Phone interview conducted with Whirlpool.

CHAPTER 4 THE FREELANCER ECONOMY

1. Intuit, "Intuit 2020 Report: Twenty Trends That Will Shape The Next Decade," October, 2010.

2. "The State of Independence in America," MBO Partners, September 2013, http://info.mbopartners.com/rs/mbo/images/2013-MBO_Partners_State_of_Independence_Report.pdf.

3. "'Online Staffing' Platform Businesses—Industry Segment Forecast Through 2020," Staffingindustry.com, January 2, 2014, www.staffingindustry.com/Research-Publications/Research-Topics/Online-Staffing.

4. Joslyn Faust, "Surveying the New World of Work: The Freelancer Model for Enterprises: Drivers and Difficulties," Tower Lane Consulting, October 2013.

5. Data was sent to me directly from Elance.

6. Data was sent to me directly from oDesk.

7. Vickie Elmer, "Freelancer Pay Jumps, in Search for Quality Work," *Fortune*, April 9, 2014.

CHAPTER 5 THE ZOOKEEPER: TODAY'S MANAGER

1. Phone interview but name had to be redacted.

2. Phone interview with Pamela Montana.

3. Gary Hamel, "First, Let's Fire All the Managers," *Harvard Business Review* (December, 2011).

4. Kelly Services, "Employee Engagement and Retention," Kelly Global Workforce Index, 2013.

CHAPTER 6 TEN PRINCIPLES OF THE FUTURE MANAGER

1. Phone interview with Whirlpool.
2. Cisco, "Cisco Global Survey Reveals That the Majority of Aspiring Executives See a Big Future for Video in the Workplace," press release, August 5, 2013, http://newsroom .cisco.com/press-release-content?type=webcontent&articleId=1233239.
3. Phone interview with Peter Aceto.
4. Phone interview with Medium.
5. Stacia Sherman Garr, "The State of Employee Recognition in 2012," Bersin & Associates, June 2012.
6. Bianca Bosker, "Sheryl Sandberg: 'There's No Such Thing As Work-Life Balance'," *Huffington Post*, April 6, 2012.
7. Steve Dent, "No Work Emails After 6PM Please, We're French," *Engadget*, April 9, 2014.
8. Robert Half, "Business Etiquette: The New Rules in a Digital Age," 2013. PDF available at www.roberthalf.com/legal/free-resources.

CHAPTER 7 THE MANAGERLESS COMPANY

1. Kevin Meyer, "No Titles Except 'Plant' Manager," January 25, 2008, http:// kevinmeyer.com/blog/2008/01/no-titles-excep.html.
2. Susan H. Greenberg, "Building Organizations That Work," August 1, 2012, www.gsb .stanford.edu/news/research/Building-Organizations-That-Work.html.

CHAPTER 8 THE ORGANIZATION OF TODAY

1. Phone interview with Thomas Friel.
2. "Employee Engagement and Retention," Kelly Global Workforce Index (2013).

CHAPTER 9 FOURTEEN PRINCIPLES OF THE FUTURE ORGANIZATION

1. Jacquelyn Smith, "The Pros and Cons of Job Hopping," *Forbes* (March 8, 2013).
2. Gallup, "State of the American Workplace," 2013. PDF available for download at www.gallup.com/strategicconsulting/163007/state-american-workplace.aspx.
3. Bradley R. Staats, Katherine L. Milkman, and Craig R. Fox, "The Team Scaling Fallacy: Underestimating the Declining Efficiency of Larger Teams" (2012).
4. Dan Schawbel, "Millennial Branding and American Express Release New Study on Gen Y Workplace Expectations," Millennial Branding, September 3, 2013.

5. Richard Branson, "Richard Branson on Intrapreneurs," *Entrepreneur Magazine* (January 31, 2011).

6. Allan Engelhardt, "The 3/2 Rule of Employee Productivity," *CYBAEA Journal* (October 16, 2006), www.cybaea.net/Blogs/employee_productivity.html.

7. Allan Engelhardt, "Employee Productivity Revisited," *CYBAEA Journal* (June 22, 2010), www.cybaea.net/Blogs/Employee-productivity-revisited.html.

8. Emily Esfahani and Jennifer L. Aaaker, "Millennial Searchers," the *New York Times*, November 30, 2013.

9. PricewaterhouseCoopers, "Unleashing the Power of Innovation," 2013.

10. Information received via email from L'Oreal.

11. Rackspace, "88 Per Cent of Cloud Users Point to Cost Savings According to Rackspace Survey," February 20, 2013, www.rackspace.com/blog/newsarticles/88-per-cent-of-cloud-users-point-to-cost-savings-according-to-rackspace-survey.

12. Catalyst, "Catalyst Quick Take: Women in U.S. Management and Labor Force," December 10, 2013, www.catalyst.org/knowledge/women-us-management-and-labor-force.

13. Viv Groksop, "If Women Had Been in Charge, Would the Economic Crisis Have Happened?" *Daily Mail,* May 8, 2009.

14. Jack Zenger and Joseph Folkman, "Are Women Better Leaders than Men?" *Harvard Business Review* (March 15, 2012).

15. Catalyst, "The Bottom Line: Corporate Performance and Women's Representation on Boards," October 15, 2007, www.catalyst.org/knowledge/bottom-line-corporate-performance-and-womens-representation-boards.

16. "Whitepaper: High Performance Entrepreneurs Women in High Tech—Summary," Illuminate Ventures, 2014, www.illuminate.com/whitepaper.

17. "What Women Want: Insights Into $7 Trillion Women's Purchasing Power," *PR Newswire,* May 28, 2013, www.prnewswire.com/news-releases/what-women-want-insights-into-7-trillion-womens-purchasing-power-209162721.html.

18. Darrell Rigby and Barbara Bilodeau, "Management Tools & Trends 2013," Bain & Company, May 8, 2013.

19. Susanne Gargiulo, "Why Everyone Wants to Work for the 'Good Guys'," *CNN*, November 8, 2012.

The FOW Community (dedicated to the future of work and collaboration)

 THE FOW COMMUNITY

The FOW Community is a "By Invitation Only," custom-built membership community dedicated to collaboration and the future of work! Future-proof your organization and improve the success rate of your collaboration initiatives. Access fresh resources that are updated regularly, and tap into a trusted network of members who not only support each other in preparing, evolving, and elevating their organizations, but also mobilize the conversations, communications, and serendipity that will shape the future of work and collaboration.

Members will be able to:

- Get access to Jacob and his team
- Share new ways of working, provide advice, and garner feedback
- Participate in public and private group discussions
- Solicit feedback about challenges and pain points
- Join groups of interest or create one of their own
- Access unique resources such as proprietary research reports, strategy whitepapers, tactical webinars, and topical case studies
- Build industry thought-leadership
- Shape the future of work and of the community
- And much more!

Members will also be able to get direct access to Jacob and his team at Chess Media Group. Visit http://www.fowcommunity.com to request an invite. If you become a member use promo code FOWBOOK for a **10 percent savings on membership fees,** available for a limited time only. Special corporate rates are available.

Index